ESCAPING THE ISLE

ESCAPING THE ISLE

A CALLIHAN CHRONICLE

BY S.N. ARNDT

MANUSCRIPTS
PRESS

ESCAPING THE ISLE
A Callihan Chronicle

ISBN

979-8-88926-513-9 *Paperback*
979-8-88926-514-6 *Ebook*

To my friends and family, thank you.

Contents

Author's Note

Hello, reader! I can't begin to say how much it means that this book has made its way to you.

This book started off in a rather unusual way. During my first year in university, I was procrastinating while studying for a midterm when I came across an advertisement for National Novel Writing Month (NaNoWriMo). I've always loved writing. Earlier that same year, I wrote part of a novel for a high school project. It seemed like a very interesting way to pass the time and, as it happened, NaNoWriMo started the same day, so I decided to get started. A plot came together quickly and, by the end of the month, I had written my very first novel. It took another year of NaNoWriMo to complete it. It wasn't long before I had come up with multiple other plots.

One of those plots was for a related story, and that story was the beginning of this book. It took more than a few years before I decided to write this. By the time I finally did, I had lived in Ireland and traveled across the country more than once, learning about the Celtic Fairy Faith, various aspects of paganism, and a number of other things that make an appearance in the book.

In all this time, I had been writing a variety of things, mostly relating to fairytales and mythologies from around the world. I had accepted that these stories were just something I would do for myself rather than actually sharing them. However, one particular evening, I felt brave and decided to submit one to a publisher.

I had always wanted to publish something, but it was always a "one day" type of thing. Maybe the glass of wine, or two, helped with that decision, or perhaps I had come to the conclusion that one day would, in fact, never come if I wasn't a little brave once in a while. Whatever it was, I remember feeling overwhelmed and proud of myself for overcoming that mental barrier. It did help that I had decided I would likely not hear back.

Imagine my surprise when I heard back and learned that my dream of publishing could be a reality! After sharing the news with my partner and our cats, I called my mom. You see, when I first told her I was going to write my very first book for that high school project, she wasn't surprised.

I thought it was a revelation, yet she just laughed and told me a story from when I was about three years old. She had come to tuck me into bed and found me in my pajamas, sitting on the bed with my eyes closed. With my face all scrunched up in thought, I shook my head and opened my eyes. She asked me about it, and my response was that I was thinking up a story and was unhappy with the people in it.

Now, that three-year-old is grown up and is overjoyed that my book has made it all the way to you. I never expected anyone would actually want to read it, let alone enjoy it. Because of that, very few people have read any of my work, let alone know more than the basic details, like the plot, before this. The fact that I was not only very wrong but that my dream is becoming a reality is both exciting and nerve-racking.

Without further ado, I hope you enjoy *Escaping the Isle: A Callihan Chronicle*!

Chapter 1

Across the world, just off the coast of Ireland, lies an island. Few go to visit, and only a few thousand reside there. It's a place the world forgot, and while time moves the same there as it does anywhere else, it feels older than it is. A land of lords and ladies, it carries few makings from the modern world, discoveries brought back from the mainland. Divided into three regions, equally powerful families rule over the land. A shaky peace is maintained by an age-old understanding, established by a queen from centuries ago.

To the eyes of the outside world, it's an ordinary place with ordinary people and very little to do there. Some remember the tales of a strange isle with strange creatures and an ancient magic among the trees. Most believe this magic never existed. While some are certain it left long ago, a few believe it still remains, and even fewer have actually seen it. This magic gave the isle its name: Isle Draíocht, Isle of Magic.

The smell of the damp woods clings to me as I run through the trees. It feels so familiar, and the feeling of freedom is so comforting. The flowers and bushes reach out toward me as I gently brush my fingertips against their soft leaves. A laugh bubbles up in my chest and escapes through my lips. It's contagious as two small rabbits hop after me. The game continues with each passing moment. They continue their chase as the tree roots move out of my way, and I climb over rocks to keep ahead. As they get closer, the white fur on the smaller one darts across the path in front of me, and I trip over a fallen branch. I gasp as the ground comes dangerously close to my face before I land on something warm and soft.

"Apologies, Miss," says a dark grey rabbit in a gravelly voice.

"You're not hurt. Are you?" the white rabbit asks with a sudden panic in its voice as I stand up, brushing my hands against my dress to remove the dirt.

"That was so much fun," I say, spinning around and giggling. I turn around to look into the trees behind. "Can we play some more, please?"

"No, child. Our time to play has passed, young Caitria," a woman with a sad smile says as she steps out from behind the large, ancient tree.

Her long hair changes colors depending on the wind, the light, and even her mood. The woman's eyes are the same, only they shift between the colors of the lake, the moss on the ground, and the bark of the trees. Her fair skin is complemented by her strange clothes. They always look as if they are made of the earth itself, with the soft moss and leaves creating her long dress and cloak. The branches at the top of her head could be a crown, but my small stature always makes it difficult to see.

"My Lady Cailleach," the white puca begins. "Perhaps the young lady can stay just a little—"

"She must be returning home now," the Cailleach interrupts with a stern voice. "You know this as well as I."

"But I don't want to," I say, stomping my foot. "I want to stay here with you and play with the pucai."

I know it's a childish reaction. If Mother saw such a display, I'd undoubtedly get a scolding. She'd say that such actions are unbecoming of a young lady, but I couldn't care less.

"Ah, yes," she says with a sigh as she kneels down to meet me at eye level. "Agatha never did care for the imagination of a child. And now she wishes for her own children to grow up as she did."

I feel tears brimming in my eyes as she brushes the leaves out of my hair with care. "Why do I have to go back?"

"Because you must be with your people, not with me and mine," the Cailleach explains softly.

She looks at me for a moment, and I see the sadness in her eyes. Even still, she's as beautiful as ever. No matter how many times I see her, I'm always reminded of the princesses in the stories Mother reads me and Enya. I almost want to ask if she is one, but I know she can't be. She may look young and beautiful at this moment, but something in me doesn't believe it. She's much more important than any princess from a storybook, though I'm not sure why. I've seen with my own eyes how she can age many years in just a few days. I stay silent, knowing she wouldn't answer my question even if I did ask. Grown-ups never do.

"But aren't you people too?" I ask, cocking my head to the side as I reach out and touch a lock of her soft hair. "You look like a person, and the pucai talk like everyone else, and I've met a lot of people."

"Do not let your eyes deceive you, child," she tells me as she stands. The wind begins to pick up as she raises her arms. The tree branches almost appear to bend and sway with the light movements of her fingers. "This world is filled with a vast number of magical things."

She gestures toward the pucai. With a light nod of her head, they both shift into different creatures. Where the rabbits once sat now stand a white wolf and a large grey raven. Fear rises up inside me at the sight of these creatures, but it's gone almost as soon as it arrives when I see their familiar bright golden eyes staring back at me. In a second, I'm overcome with delight as I walk over to them to feel the wolf's soft fur. I bury my face in the raven's soft feathers as I hear her lightly laugh.

"Dear Caitria, you mustn't let your eyes trick you into thinking we are of the same world," she says, gesturing toward the pucai, who bows back at her in response. "And your world is one you very much need to return to."

"Oh, all right," I say as I step away from them all. She's told me this many times, and I know there's no use in arguing. The ground behind me clears, creating a path away from the massive, ancient tree. "Goodbye then," I say with a reluctant wave.

"Until we meet again, child," I hear her voice say, seeming to come from everywhere around me.

The pucai join me on my walk back, having transitioned back into rabbits. They maintain a short distance behind me, and I know it's because of the fear the people have for them. I've been warned about the forest as long as I can remember. Warnings to never trust the pucai, scraggly shapeshifting creatures with golden eyes, fell on deaf ears. They've only ever been companions and friends to me.

The walk back feels long, but the plants and roots at my feet always seem to make way for me whenever I go through. Like magic, the path always leads me to where I want to go. The wildflowers scattered around reach out toward me, and I admire their beautiful petals along the way. I look back and catch a glimpse of two pairs of golden eyes, but the path I've been walking, as always, has overgrown in a matter of seconds. There aren't many twists and turns, but it's always dark.

The only light in this part of the forest are the will-o'wisps that dance through the trees at night. Their pale blue light shines down, casting beautiful yet ominous shadows along the ground. It's a magical sight that always disappears the closer I get to the edge of the woods.

As I make my way through the trees, I realize Mother will be quite cross with me at the dirt on my clothing. The only comfort I find in the walk back to Callihan Manor is the rustling of leaves from behind me. While the pucai can only show themselves in the night or around the woman at the old tree, they always make sure I'm safe while in the forest.

The glimpses of light out of the corner of my eyes let me know that, even at seven years old, I am capable of taking care of myself. Even with the lack of dangerous animals in our remote part of the world, the pucai will continue to watch over me just in case.

Before I know it, the leaves rustling behind me begin to grow silent, and lights begin to shine through the trees as I near the edge of the forest. As I come out of the tree line and emerge from over the hill, I see a young woman waving at me from the garden gate. I rush down to her, completely ignoring Mother's voice in my head that says ladies should never run anywhere. As I get closer to the wooden gate at the bottom of the hill, I can see the look of fear in her eyes as she sees me, dirty clothes and all. I'm about to reach her when I wake up.

Chapter 2

Rubbing the sleep from my eyes, I look over at the clock to see that it's almost time to wake up. With a sigh, I swing my legs off the bed and brace myself for the cold wood floor of my bedroom. Even though I've just woken up, I'm already exhausted for the day to come. I walk over to the closet and swing open the door to find a set of clothes hanging just inside—a boring dark brown skirt with a buttoned blouse and what Mother would call "sensible" shoes.

Making the quick trip across the room to my small private bathroom, I shower and brush my teeth, allowing myself a brief moment to reminisce about the memory I'd just woken up from. I wash my face, catching a glimpse of my dark green eyes staring back at me in the small mirror. The dark circles under my eyes only stand as a reminder of how tired I am.

It's been nearly ten years since I was last able to leave the manor freely. The pucai, will-o'wisps, and the Cailleach all were just stories until, one day, they weren't. And the tales didn't tell the full story either. The woman who is supposed to be a cold, calculating faerie queen never acted that way toward me, and the mischievous and tricky pucaí only ever protected me from my own boredom. The only part that was right was the will-o'wisps, who lit up the darkest areas of the forest near the ancient faerie tree.

As time passed, I began to make connections between what I remember and the stories around the isle. Shannon, our cook, told me about the strange creatures and beings in the forest behind the manor, and Mother even read some of the tales to Enya and me when we were little. Even as a child, I knew something was different about my experiences.

My recounting of them was always written off as stories from a child's imagination. Shannon was the only one who seemed to believe me. However, so many years have passed that I'm beginning to think everyone was actually right. Perhaps they were just stories I had made up to cure my boredom.

Three quick, perfunctory knocks draw me out of my thoughts. My stomach clenches as I steel myself for what I know will be an unpleasant interaction. With an internal sigh, I fix a smile on my face as I open the bathroom door an inch to find Mother's face glaring at me.

"How are you not ready, you lazy child? If you don't hurry yourself, we'll be late to the fitting," Mother says with a sharp tone, her shrewd brown eyes gleaming with displeasure. She pauses a moment before adding, "And you know how I hate to be late."

"Yes, Mother," I say in a docile voice that I have long since perfected. "I'll only be a moment longer."

"Very good," she says with a pleased smile. "You must make a good impression. Brigit McNeillain may have known you since your infancy, but that does not mean you can be careless. You are expected to act in a manner befitting of our family."

"Yes, Mother," I say as I emerge freshly cleaned from the bathroom.

Walking over to the clothes left hanging on the closet door, I quickly slip them on before grabbing a pin to tame my wild dark brown, waist-length hair. I wrap it around my hand before twisting it up and back and pinning it into a secure bun.

"I don't intend to make a negative impression, nor do I intend to give our family a reputation of being tardy." I grab the makeup on my vanity and throw on a few quick swipes of mascara. "The new seamstress asked that we arrive on time, and I plan to respect her request."

"Very good, Caitria. Perhaps you'll finally start acting like a lady," Mother says, and I can hear a hint of pride in her voice. A frown of disgust quickly takes its place when I turn to look at her. "Honestly, Caitria, you look absolutely ghastly. How many times do I have to tell you? You must rise with the sun to look rested. But I suppose there's nothing to be done about it now."

I hold my tongue, remaining silent as I look down at the photo on the small bedside table. The young girl looks up with a bright smile. Her wild dark reddish-brown hair and green eyes are identical to mine. No matter how harsh Mother's words, I must remember Enya.

My poor little sister deserves nothing more than to enjoy her life free from criticism. I'm exhausted already, but I know that, even at seventeen, Mother expects me to act every bit the lady that she's willed me to be. I know if her focus remains on me, her harsh words won't find a new target.

"Now that you're *finally* ready, let us go into town," Mother says with a huff as she leaves my room.

I take a deep, calming breath before I venture into the entry hall, closing the door behind me. It takes no more than two minutes to descend the staircase, but Mother has already entered the car and is impatiently waiting for me. I give our butler and chauffeur, Alan, a smile in thanks as he holds the door open for me.

"Now, remember," Mother says, inspecting her bracelet as I slide in beside her. "Brigit will treat you as though you are her daughter. With the wedding so close, she's simply ensuring you are appropriate to represent both her family and ours."

"Yes, Mother," I reply as I look out the window, quietly hoping beyond hope that this won't be a painful experience.

Shades of green and brown inch by as we exit the stone gate and go toward the main road leading into our small town. The forest can be seen in the distance but is hidden at times by sheep and the occasional farm until, eventually, it's completely out of sight. Several orchards pass by the window, the trees bare as the chill of winter has just recently arrived.

Short stone walls divide the land of our people, and slightly taller wooden fences define the three regions. With Isle Draíocht being divided between the Callihan, McNeillain, and Hadden families, the only way for one family to reign over the others was simple. Two families needed to become one, and Seamus McNeillain and I were the perfect children to make that dream a reality.

We were thrown into the power struggle, and there wasn't anything we could do about it. The Hadden family always found our relationship difficult to believe, especially Gerald, who'd grown up with us. However, we played our parts so perfectly that no one even questioned when Seamus proposed on my seventeenth birthday.

I know that if I were to look out Mother's window to the east, I'd see Hadden Manor. After a minute, I can begin to see McNeillain Manor to the west past a wooden fence. A wave of anxiety and fear settle in my stomach at the sight of the grand estate, even at a distance. Soon, I'll live there with Seamus and his family. The thought plagues my mind. I force myself to ignore such thoughts, instead focusing on the positives—the few that remain, at least.

Soon, short single and two-story buildings block my view as we enter the outskirts of the town. I've seen it all many times before, each time wondering, *Why in the world am I not allowed to go here on my own?* Ever since turning thirteen, I've been forbidden to go into town on my own. It never was and never will be for safety reasons, but instead to force me to distance myself from the people. Even children are allowed to walk or ride their bicycles into town. Teenagers my age make it an event to go into town together.

Almost as if I manifested it, a few people stand talking and laughing outside O'Shaughnessy's pub as we pass through the center of town. How I wish I could be among them, but I know such a thought isn't realistic. A small sigh escapes my lips before I realize it.

"Ladies, do not stare out the window of cars and sigh, Caitria," Mother snaps while pointedly looking at me out of the corner of her eye. She scoffs at the sight of the people outside the pub, casting them a look of disdain.

"My apologies," I quietly say as I straighten up and look down at my hands.

"Caitria," Mother says with a warning tone. "You are a future lady of Isle Draíocht. You must act like it. No one will respect you if you act with such frivolity." She gestures toward the teenagers. "Such behavior is disgraceful. And it is most certainly not becoming of anyone of our position."

"I know, Mother," I say quietly.

Even after hearing her harsh words for years, they still sting. And no matter what, Mother always finds something wrong with every single thing I do.

"We've arrived, Lady Callihan," Alan says in his usual calm, even voice as he opens Mother's door.

We both get out of the car in front of the seamstress's shop. While Mother walks right in with a wide smile, I only feel a wave of nausea come over me as I look up at the sign. Its neat lettering reads: *O'Grady's Tailor Shop.*

"I'm sure you'll look beautiful, Lady Caitria," I hear Alan say from behind me.

I give him a small smile as I mentally prepare myself. Glancing down the way, I can almost hear the water at the port not too far from here. While I'd like nothing more than to avoid this place, I can't. I take a deep breath, trying to calm my nerves as I walk inside.

As soon as we enter the shop, it's clear that Mab O'Grady has been excitedly awaiting our arrival. Her bright smile is practically contagious. A few years older than me and slightly shorter, her hands are clasped together, resting under her chin. Her light brown hair is thrown up into a clip haphazardly, and I feel a bit sorry for her as I see her hands shaking. She's probably extremely nervous about this as well. If our appointment goes well, she'll have solidified her position as the seamstress for both the Callihan and McNeillain families.

"Welcome, Lady Callihan and young Lady Caitria," she says in an excited voice, bowing her head toward us with a slight curtsy. "I'm so happy you have arrived! Lady McNeillain has only just arrived herself,"

"Yes, thank you, Mab," Brigit McNeillain says as she walks out of the back room.

Brigit's hair is pulled back in a twist identical to Mother's, only exacerbating the frown lines that've permanently formed on her face. Even from here, the smell of whiskey overpowers her pungent sour perfume.

Brigit gives me a small nod as she takes in my appearance. With a frown and not much else, she immediately starts whispering to Mother as they both walk toward the back of the shop. Mab quickly follows behind them, and I use this brief moment of being forgotten to take in the shop.

The first thing I notice is that the shop is completely spotless, and nothing seems even the slightest bit out of place. A collection of fabric rolls hangs on the wall, and a small table holds a variety of hats, belts, and other accessories that one might wear on a daily basis. Mannequins stand at the two small front windows, showing some of Mab's latest creations. On the right side of the shop, the female mannequin is wearing a simple skirt and a blouse, similar to my own clothes. The male one wears a basic pair of trousers and a button-down.

The left side of the shop is remarkably different. The fabrics on the wall shine and glitter. A table of accessories, ties, sashes, and what appear to be fancy buttons are expertly displayed. The mannequins in the window are dressed for a lavish event. A strapless dark green dress with a full skirt is accompanied by a thin shawl on one of the figures. The other is dressed to the nines in a coat and tails, complete with a top hat and a scarf.

"Caitria," Mother snaps.

I look toward the back where the three women have gathered and find them all watching me. Mother, hiding an angry expression, gestures for me to join them. I hurry toward them as the room opens up to reveal a large, plush lounge chair against the side wall with a small table in front of it. Biscuits and tea have been set out for Mother and Brigit. Mab pours them each a cup as they settle in before glancing over at me.

"Would you like a cuppa?" she asks me with a kind smile.

"No, she wouldn't," Brigit replies for me, her dark eyes glaring at me. "With the wedding so soon, too much tea will make it harder for her to start a family right away."

My face goes hot at her response, and I want to disappear. No matter how embarrassing and uncomfortable it is, I keep my thoughts to myself. While it's not the first time I've heard such a thing from her, this is the first time she's openly talked about children in front of anyone other than Mother and me.

"O-of course," Mab stutters, clearly not expecting such a blunt comment. "If you'll follow me, please," she says as she gestures into the dressing room at the opposite end of the room.

As soon as Mab flicks the curtains closed, I can hear the faint sound of whispering voices. Not even wanting to take the effort to decipher what they could possibly be criticizing, my eyes focus on the subject of today's excursion. Hanging on the wall between a tall, narrow mirror and a small stool is a black bag I can only assume to be the rumored wedding dress.

Even the sight of the bag makes me anxious. Mother and Brigit insisted on being part of the design process. As a result, I had absolutely no voice in the matter. Even though it was months ago, I cringe at the memory. Mother and Brigit didn't bother to whisper about my "unsavory" measurements. As soon as she was done, Mab was quickly whisked away by Mother and Brigit to discuss the design of my wedding dress. But, rather than dwell on something I know can't change at this point, I focus on the task at hand.

After slipping out of my clothing and folding it into a neat pile on the stool, Mab helps me gingerly step into the center of the white mound of fabric that she's arranged on the floor.

"Just take a moment if ya need it, and then I'll pull it up, yeah?" she says softly.

I nod as a wave of nausea flows over me. As she carefully pulls the dress up, I feel my throat tighten as sadness overwhelms me. I had longed to marry for love, but as Mother would say, such thoughts are unbecoming for someone of my standing. Once it's high enough for me to get my arms through the sleeves, I close my eyes to keep the tears from forming. Mab buttons up the back of the dress, and I open my eyes and glance over to see my reflection in the mirror.

The dress itself is a bright white, a stark contrast to my own dark hair and green eyes. It's heavier than I expected with all the lace details, but the large satin skirt and long train bunched up behind me provides some indication of just how much fabric there actually is. The shape of the skirt looks like a large bell and is complemented by the semi-poofy sleeves. Pearls decorate the high neckline, along the edge of the sleeves and, at a quick glance, along the bottom of the dress as well.

All things considered, the dress is far from what I had expected. After the comments Mother and Brigit have made about how my dress will never live up to the beauty and glory of their own gowns, I'm surprised by how nice it looks. While it's not what I had dreamed of as a child, it's more than acceptable. As Mab opens the curtains and guides me to a small, round platform in the center of the room, I hear them gasp.

"It looks like we can take in some of the waist," Mab mumbles to herself as she grabs a wristband with pins from one of the many hooks on the back wall. "And the sleeves are a touch too long."

"What is this?" I hear Mother demand as Mab is just about to pin one of the sleeves. Mother and Brigit were clearly expecting something else. I look over to Mab, whose face has gone bright red, the pins now forgotten.

"Well, you see," Mab begins, clearly having something rehearsed. "This dress has elements of what you had requested. If you would allow me to—"

"What's the meaning of this?" Brigit demands, completely ignoring the fact that Mab just spoke.

"This is not what we had discussed," says Mother as her voice rises. "Where is the dress we designed?"

"Please," Mab says with her hands clasped in front of her. "Please calm down and—"

"You ask us to calm down, yet I don't see the dress we requested!" Mother exclaims. Mab begins to shrink away from the power in Mother's voice. "Are you trying to make a mockery of our family? Because you are certainly succeeding."

"What about my family?" Brigit shrieks. "That girl is marrying my son, but she won't be doing it in this monstrosity you call a dress!"

"I want an explanation, and I want one now," Mother bellows. At this point, it's clear Mab is second-guessing her choices.

"This dress is very similar to the one we discussed," Mab begins in a calm voice, and I can tell she clearly prepared for the worst-case scenario that has just unfolded. "The pearl details are here, and the long sleeves," she explains as she points to different parts of the dress. "The lace details are there too, though the pattern looks slightly different." The women share a look but, surprisingly, stay silent as Mab continues.

"The minor changes I made were to accommodate a style that would fit Lady Caitria's figure best," she says but is interrupted before she can say anything else.

"Oh, who cares what the girl looks like?" Brigit snaps and crosses her arms as she looks at me with disgust.

I pretend not to notice the venom in her words, choosing instead to focus on the wall behind their heads.

"The dress is hideous, and she's certainly not one to turn heads anyway."

"What Lady McNeillain is trying to say," Mother chimes in with a sharp tone, and I flinch slightly. "Is that the girl's figure is of no importance. We know what she'll look best in, and as the seamstress, you shouldn't have changed the design."

"The slight modifications are also in line with the current fashion trends on the mainland. You requested she look regal and respectable.

What better way to do that than in a dress that's in the latest styles?" Mab explains, quickly changing her tactic.

Mother and Brigit sit there, silently thinking. It feels like they're overreacting, which would come as no surprise. Mother has been known to throw a fit if the butter isn't the right temperature, and Brigit is no better. I can practically see the wheels turning in their heads as they try to figure out how to get their way.

"Is there time to remake it?" Mother asks after sharing another look at Brigit.

"It takes at least a month for the fabric to come in," Mab responds. "And even if I had the materials and worked through the night, every night, until the wedding, there wouldn't be time to redo everything."

"Very well," Mother says after a tense moment, and Mab lets out a faint yet audible breath of relief.

Mother and Brigit share a quick glance, and I can see their thoughts written on their faces. In their minds, Seamus and I have to get married as soon as possible. The sooner we're married, the sooner they have more power and control over the isle.

"Quite right, Agatha," Brigit nods with a forced smile. "Perhaps the right veil will salvage our vision."

"I have several options for you to choose from," Mab says as she turns around.

She gives me a small wink before grabbing two options from one of the many hooks along the wall. As she brings them over to Mother and Brigit, I realize that the changes she made to the design might not have been for the reasons she said but rather because they're something she thought I would like. Regardless of whether that is true or not, I feel quite touched at the possibility.

Throughout this entire process, I've never once been asked about what I want. As they select veils for me to try on, I let my mind wander. After all, all I really need to do is stand on the platform and remain still so Mother and Brigit can see what each and every veil option looks like with the dress.

Every single thought that enters my mind, however, only shows the depressing reality of my situation. I feel tears prickle my eyes, and I quickly blink them away while a particularly thick veil is covering my face. The only person who understands this sorrow is Seamus, and we're stuck in this sinking ship together. My dearest friend, he's the brother I never had. At the very least, we'll be in this farce together. That thought is both lonely and comforting.

Chapter 3

By the time the appointment ends, Mother directs Alan to take us back to the manor. She and Father have an important meeting with the McNeillains and the Haddens that I'm not allowed to attend. Thankfully, that means I'm left at the manor for the rest of the evening. They leave without a word almost as soon as we arrive. The second I see the car pass through the stone gate, I feel a sense of relief. I finally have a moment to breathe, knowing no one here would report back to them. My first stop is the kitchen, where I know Shannon must be.

I can hear her even before I get halfway down the hall. Shannon is talking and laughing as the giggle of a young girl floats into the hallway. A smile forms as I know that sound. Such joy warms my heart, especially in a manor that always feels so cold.

I round the corner and see Shannon kneading dough at the large counter in the center of the room while her daughter, Cecilia, sits and colors on the opposite side. The warmth from the wood-fire stove at one end of the room seeps into my bones as I walk inside. Almost as soon as I step foot into the space, Cecilia squeals in delight and climbs down from her chair, dragging me by the hand over to sit next to her.

"How was it, Miss Caitria?" four-year-old Cecilia asks me while I draw outlines of shapes for her color. "Did ya look like a faerie princess?"

"I almost did," I tell her with a smile. I glance over at the cabinets at the far end of the room, where a variety of containers fill the counter. The herbs hanging from the wire overhead release a subtle aroma. I close my eyes for a second and breathe in the comforting scent before going back to coloring.

"How could ya *almost* look like a faerie princess?" Cecilia asks as she colors the sheep I just outlined. With her imagination and coloring skills, it has green fur and bright red eyes. "Ya either look like one or ya don't," she tells me matter-of-factly.

"Well, I could certainly imagine a faerie wearing the dress I had on, but I look nothing like one," I tell her. In that moment, Enya bounds in with a wide smile.

"Caitria!" she happily exclaims as she throws her arms around me in a warm hug. I hug her back before she sits down to join us. "How was the shop? Did you look beautiful in your dress?"

"Of course she did," Shannon tuts in response as she rubs her pregnant belly, letting the dough rest. "Your sister is one of the most beautiful girls on the isle. I'm sure her wedding dress is just as beautiful as she is, especially with Mab's talent."

Seven years older than me, Shannon, several months pregnant with her second child, brings Cecilia into work when her family is unable to watch her. Shannon's glowing with happiness, her green eyes practically sparkling, especially around her young daughter. At times like these, I can pretend I'm from a normal family with an ordinary life, not one of the future rulers of the isle. While I envy her and her happiness, I know I have to do what's demanded of me.

"You're right about that, Miss Shannon," Enya dreamily sighs as she twists a lock of hair around her finger.

"She'll be a faerie!" Cecilia exclaims, and I glance over at Enya to see the hurt hiding behind her eyes.

Mother refused to let her join us, even after begging her for weeks.

"I agree." Enya laughs as she gets up off the stool.

She grabs Cecilia by her small hands and spins around with her as both of them start giggling. Shannon and I laugh with them as Enya snags a towel with her free hand and puts it around her waist like a skirt as she spins the young girl around. She begins to hum along to an imaginary tune as they dance. It's a combination of a few songs, the notes all over the place, but Cecilia begins to hum along to her own tune. Their hodge-podge song is a jumble of sounds and only increases their joy.

Not even a moment later, the soft crackling sound of a radio begins. Shannon only ever brings out the radio whenever Mother and Father are out. They've always been against anyone in the manor having such "modern contraptions" for entertainment, so it's always a treat whenever we get to listen to the music from the mainland. Enya squeals in excitement and turns up the music as Cecilia continues jumping around in circles.

"All the way from America, that was The B-52s' new single, 'Love Shack,'" The radio announcer says through the soft crackling of the speakers. "Now, let's listen to one of our favorite hits, The Pogues and The Dubliners' 'The Irish Rover.'"

Cecilia happily shrieks as Enya dances around with her. Cecilia's light brown curls bounce as she giggles at Enya's antics. Their laughter is contagious, and Enya's makeshift skirt tips things over the edge of absurdity. They each grab one of my hands and begin to dance around in a circle. Joining in, I let myself just have fun and enjoy the moment. We take turns spinning each other and skillfully distract Cecilia whenever she begins to look over at Shannon, who's still experiencing morning sickness even at five months pregnant.

I feel myself laughing along with them as Shannon looks on, smiling at the three of us. The song fades, and the crackling from the cold wind outside takes over enough so we can barely hear the announcer.

I find myself wishing, not for the first time today, that this much happiness had been at the shop instead of the tense judgment that plagued my appointment. My laughter dies at that thought, and I notice Enya glancing over at me with a questioning look.

"Cecilia," Shannon says, and their laughter fades away to listen. "Sweetie, can you go out to the garden with Miss Enya and gather some berries and herbs for mummy?"

"Can Miss Caitria come too?" she asks as she grabs my hand. "She always finds the best things."

"No, love," Shannon says as she tucks a loose curl behind her ear. "I need Miss Caitria to help me with a few things in here while you two do that."

"Oh, all right." Cecilia sighs before rushing out the door, completely forgetting her warm coat on the hook by the garden door at the back of the kitchen.

Enya trails behind her, grabbing both of their coats and making sure she doesn't fall over the step down into the garden just beyond the door. Almost as soon as the door shuts behind them, Shannon places a gentle arm around my shoulders as I look down at my hands. I find I can't look away from them. The same hands will have a wedding band soon, and I feel my throat close at what that would mean. No matter how hard I try to ignore the sadness and defeat that fills my heart at the thought, it never goes away.

"Seamus is a good man, dearie," Shannon says in a warm and comforting voice. "He'll be a good husband."

"I know," I say, and I can hear just how shaky my breathing is. "I just wish we weren't forced into this."

"I know," she says as she pulls me into a hug as tears begin forming in my eyes. "I know. And who knows? You've already got a good friendship, so perhaps love isn't far off."

"Maybe," I say with a sad and resigned sigh. "But it's just wishful thinking at this point."

"You do care for him, yeah?" Shannon retorts, and I can clearly tell she is trying to make me feel more optimistic about the situation. A few tears begin to fall, and I wipe them away with my sleeve.

"Yes," I say, knowing she's grasping at what little hope there is in this hopeless situation.

"Well, that's something then!" she exclaims, ever the optimist.

"But it isn't, though," I reply miserably as she pats my hand for a small way of comfort.

"And why not?" Shannon responds with her hands on her hips.

"Seamus and I are more like siblings than anything," I tell her. "He's like a brother to me, and I know he feels the same way. We're not like you and Finn."

"Well, my husband is pretty lucky." She smiles with a small chuckle. Even hearing Finn's name is enough to make Shannon glow with love and happiness. "I'm certain it won't be as bad as you think," she says after a very brief moment. "Are you sure he doesn't love you, though? He could be hiding it."

"There's no way he could hide that," I say, shaking my head at the thought. "We're practically related at this point. That much hasn't ever changed. And it's not like I think it'll be bad." I sigh.

"I always thought they'd change their minds after a few years. Maybe they'd realize that our friendship is more than enough to be good leaders, and we don't need to be married to work together." I hear my voice crack as my throat tightens, and I can feel the tears forming once again.

"I'm so sorry, Cait," she whispers as she gives me a tight hug. "If I could change things, I promise I would."

"Thanks," I say as I blink away the tears and stand up. She gives me a sad smile and a hug before giving me a small nod of support as she places her hands on my shoulders. "At least we won't be going through it alone."

"No, certainly not." Shannon sighs as Cecilia's laughter floats in from the garden outside. "Why don't you make your way to bed? I'll send Alan up with some tea and biscuits a little later."

"That would be lovely," I say in thanks.

As I walk out of the kitchen and up the stairs to my room, all I want to do is cry. A lump forms in my throat, and tears prick my eyes at the realization that the joy in that kitchen will be a rarity. I can only watch from the outside after the wedding. It'll never be my reality.

Chapter 4

Not long after I got to my room, I changed into my sleep clothes and crawled under the blankets. My mind spins, and it feels like only a second has gone by before I hear Alan knock to let me know he's leaving a tray just outside the door. I wait a moment to make sure he's left before opening it to pull the small roller tray into my room.

As promised, Shannon has sent up some tea and biscuits. After rolling the tray over toward the window overlooking the lake behind the manor and the forest in the distance, I mischievously smile as I pour myself a cup of tea, remembering Brigit's comment about children from the seamstress shop. I pull the comfortable chair away from the corner of the room and set it up next to the tray before settling in with a warm blanket.

I sip my cup of tea as the sun slowly sinks behind the trees. Night has fallen quickly this winter evening as the sky blooms with pinks and purples. It's so peaceful, and I allow myself a moment to take in the beauty of the isle. A few fruit trees can be seen in the corner of my view on the far end of the lake. A few small hills block my sight of the farms and homes, but the occasional smoke billowing up in columns from the lit fireplaces reminds me that our people are always there. It's a subtle reminder that, even when I'm alone, I won't ever be able to ignore my future.

My tea grows cold as I munch on one of Shannon's honey short-bread biscuits and watch the sky shift and change. I'm not a lady of Draíocht yet, and there's no way I'm letting my own thoughts get in the way of one of my last peaceful nights before my entire life changes. Soon enough, stars begin to pepper the sky, and I sigh contentedly. Simple moments like this—when the world fades away and my responsibilities and duties are diminished to nothing more than a passing thought—really keep me sane.

Maybe things won't be so bad, I think, trying to find some optimism. *As long as Seamus and I remain friends and Enya can live happily, maybe my life won't feel so confining and suffocating.*

Soon, however, more realistic thoughts fill my mind as I look toward the trees of the forest and feel the same sense of longing I've always felt. I want to run back to the magic of the woods, to where I spent so much time as a child. I want to speak with the Cailleach and run through the trees freely with the pucai. But even thinking this, I struggle to believe such things even existed.

It feels so childish to still have even a speck of belief in fairytales. If Mother were to ever know I had hope that such things were real, she'd slap me without hesitation. I can practically hear her voice in my head and feel the stinging of my cheek.

Grow up, Caitria, she'd say. *How could a child of mine believe those old stories were real?*

Regardless of how real it actually was, it felt real to me, and I still long for that magic and the freedom that came with it. Even if it was only my imagination, I treasure that happiness. A warmth blooms in my chest as I remember the laughter and joy that came with those memories. Hours of fun without a care in the world that now only exist in my memories. Tears begin to form in my eyes as that warmth grows cold and cruel.

The happiness I felt there, that I felt as a child, has now been replaced with the weight of a forced marriage and the responsibility of being the next lady of Draíocht. In a way, it truly feels like the light and life has been slowly seeping out of me. Day by day, I feel like I am becoming more of a broken shell of a person, barely held together by sheer will and fake smiles. I let the tears fall freely and cry silently at this life I've been forced into.

In the end, I know it will just be me in this strange gilded cage I've been forced in. While beautiful and comfortable, it'll also be full of sadness and void of love and opportunities. That will be my reality. At the very least, I will never be completely alone. Seamus will be right there with me, and I feel some solace in that. We may never love one another, but at least we'll trust each other.

After a tear falls into my cold tea, I decide I need to calm down. As soon as the tears slow, I realize I'm trying to put on a fake calmness even while alone. It really is crushing to realize that even though there's no one here, I'm trying to play the part of the perfect lady they've forced me into. I feel like I really have lost myself. I'm a molded shell of a person that I don't want to be, and I never really got the chance to find who I am. Instead, I'm now the puppet of a perfect lady, future daughter-in-law of the McNeillains, and ruler for the people on the isle.

I feel as if years of exhaustion have fallen onto my shoulders, and suddenly I'm drained. I finally place the mug I've been holding on to the tray next to the now-empty plate of biscuits. I stand up and am about to turn away from the window when I see a flash of white out of the corner of my eye.

Curious, I set the blanket down on the chair and step up to the glass to get a better view. What I see nearly knocks the breath from my lungs. The white light I saw before is zipping back and forth between the tree trunks at the edge of the forest. My curiosity is overwhelming. It looks nothing like the light from a lantern or torch, and doesn't appear to flicker in the slightest.

I know I shouldn't, especially with Mother's habit of barging into my room at the first light of dawn, but curiosity gets the better of me. The overwhelming urge to go to the forest pushes me to move a bit more quickly. I've ignored the feeling so many times in the past, but tonight, on one of my last nights before the wedding, I decide to throw caution to the wind and go.

I throw on a warm sweater and slip on a pair of shoes as a wave of excitement flows through me. I quietly make my way down the stairs and into the kitchen, making sure to avoid the creaky floorboards the entire way. One glance around the room lets me know that the rest of the manor is asleep. After unlatching the back door leading to the garden, I slip outside.

I breathe in the chilly damp air and smile at the sensation before hurrying up the hill. As I get to the top of the hill, however, I begin to question my decision. It was impulsive and, while I've never felt in danger near the trees, I'm suddenly hit with the reality of the fact that it's been almost ten years since I've been anywhere near the forest. I'm about to turn back when I feel a tug, almost like an invisible rope, pulling me toward the tree line.

Soon, I'm just a few feet away from the trees. At that moment, I notice two pairs of bright golden eyes staring back at me. Their sudden appearance almost makes me scream, but I keep quiet at the last second. Mother has struck me for less. Fear races through me as the hair on the back of my neck stands up. My palms grow sweaty, and I'm about to turn and run back when the eyes vanish, and I hear a whisper of familiar voices. My thoughts stop, and I freeze in place to listen. However familiar, the voices sound muffled, almost like I'm hearing them through water.

I take a few steps closer, and the voices become a little louder. When I pass the first few trees, I feel a soft pop in my head, and I can hear the voices, clear as day.

"Does she remember us?" one gravelly voice asks. "Why does she look scared?"

"She came all the way here, did she not?" the other responds.

I step in the direction of the voices and see faint lights coming from two small rabbits hiding in the bushes, who appear to be in deep conversation. The leaves move aside slightly, allowing me to see them more clearly.

"She did, but that could mean she was just curious," the white one retorts and then sighs. "I knew I shouldn't have summoned her here."

"She was always a curious child," the grey one says. "Anyway, I highly doubt your jumping through the trees did anything to bring her here. It was the Cailleach's magic that—"

They both stop talking and look up at me as I gasp. I take a few steps back but trip over my own feet and begin to fall. However, before I hit the ground, something soft cushions my fall.

"Was she always so clumsy?" the white one asks with a giggle. "She felt different earlier, but just now, she felt like herself."

"Be quiet, you daft goblin," the grey one snaps. "She's afraid of us! Look at her. The poor girl is so scared she's crying."

"What?" I mumble as I touch my cheeks.

Sure enough, my fingers are damp from tears. This makes me come to my senses, and I stand up. I look down at what caught me and am surprised to see a tree root sinking beneath the earth and the moss on the ground around it shrinking back into the ground. I watch in shock as it soon disappears completely. Before I can process that, I feel something nudge against my leg. I look down to find the white rabbit looking up at me with a paw resting on my leg.

"Have you truly forgotten everything?" it asks sadly. "It's been so long, yet we had hoped you'd remember us."

"Is this real?" I mumble, more to myself than anyone. I reach toward the puca and feel its soft fur under my fingertips. The sensation is unexpected and makes me jump, but it also overwhelms me to the point that my legs give out from under me, and I collapse to the ground. "How is this real?"

"We're as real today as we were when you were smaller," The grey one says, perching itself on a rock in front of me.

"It's so nice to see you," I say after a moment.

My voice sounds shaky, and the deep breath I take to try and calm down does little to help. Joy, sorrow, and confusion flood my mind as I process the fact that these creatures, who protected me and who were some of my closest friends as a child, actually exist. "I'm sorry it's been so long."

"Think nothing of it," the white one says as it gives me a very human-looking smile, showing off its jagged teeth. It's a sight to behold, and while slightly disturbing, it's also endearing and comforting. Its smile fades after a moment as it watches me. It comes close enough to touch my cheek with its paw.

"It has been so long since we last saw you, young Caitria," the white one says with a hint of sadness as it removes its paw from my face. "Sorrow has clouded your Sight."

"Come with us," the grey one says in a serious voice. "There's something you must see."

They both wait patiently as I stand up. Once I do, they begin walking, making sure to never stray too far from the tree line.

"Where are you taking me?" I ask after a few minutes.

Both pucai stop and look at me before sharing a look and remaining silent. They continue walking. A few more minutes go by, and I begin to hear the sound of crunching leaves and twigs snapping mixed with metal creaking. As we get closer, I try to puzzle together what exactly they're planning to show me. Moments later, we come to a small clearing, and I see the source of the sound.

Standing in the middle of the clearing is a young lady. Her hair is pulled back into a ponytail, and I can see her round face in the light of the moon. I recognize her from somewhere but can't quite place her. In the moonlight, she looks nervous as she continually pulls at the sleeves of the sweater that hangs off her figure. Leaning against one of the trees behind her is an old bicycle.

I hear another set of footsteps in the distance, coming closer, and my heart fills with dread. I can't explain why, but something doesn't feel right about this at all. A twig snaps, and I turn my head toward the sound, confused to see someone else.

From this distance, I can't quite see who it is, though it's very clearly a man. I'm instantly on high alert. A young woman, alone at night, could be in danger. My stomach sinks as I come to this realization. However, as they get closer to the small clearing, I begin to see more of their features.

When I realize that the dark reddish hair and strong, slim build belong to none other than my fiancé, Seamus, I'm extremely confused and concerned. I know Seamus would never hurt anyone, but something feels very wrong about this entire situation.

"Seamus?" I say, unable to stop myself. "What are you doing here?"

To my surprise, however, he keeps walking toward the clearing.

"Seamus," I say again as he continues. "What're you doing?"

Again, I get no reaction from him. I look at the young woman and notice that she's not moved at all. There's no indication that either one heard me. I'm about to say something else when the grey puca places a paw on my leg to stop me.

"They cannot see nor hear us," the white puca tells me.

"The Cailleach has shielded us from their senses. As long as we remain behind the trees, we are observers," the grey one continues.

I nod and stand there, watching in confusion and curiosity.

Chapter 5

I watch silently as the young woman rushes to him and wraps her arms around his neck. He holds her close, and I can hear his muffled voice say something in her ear before letting her go. Her smile jogs my memory. I met Darina Fitzpatrick a few years ago during the Samhain festival. She was one of the kindest people and was always smiling, making sure that all of the children were able to finish their pumpkin carvings before the sun set.

"I started to think you wouldn't come," she says with a relieved sigh, her shoulders visibly relaxing.

"We don't have much time left," Seamus responds after a moment, his voice heavy with emotion. "I won't let any more time go to waste, Darina."

"I know," she says with a sad smile as she rests her head against his chest.

He holds her once more as the realization hits me like a ton of bricks. A mix of sadness and joy fills my heart as I continue watching them.

"We can't meet anymore," Seamus says softly.

"How did things turn out like this?" Darina says, her voice cracking with sadness.

"I don't know. We didn't plan for this to happen," Seamus tries to comfort her, his voice shaking.

"Maybe if we hadn't met, we could've avoided this," Darina says, her voice wavering. "It's a cruel twist of fate."

"Hey, now. I wouldn't have ever known what it's like to be in love if it weren't for you," Seamus says as the moonlight shines off the tears on his face. "It may hurt, but I wouldn't change one second."

My breath catches in my throat at his words, and I feel like the world is closing in around me. My mind spins, and I'm having a hard time breathing as my heartbeat quickens. It's like everything I thought I knew about Seamus wasn't ever true. While reluctant, he always seemed to have the same resigned acceptance of our engagement. I had no idea that he had found someone.

I can't even imagine what must be going through his head. The fact that he knew the risks of what might happen if word got back to our parents, yet he still fell in love with her, tells me just how much he cares for her. Our parents wouldn't do anything openly, but they would never let something like this go without hurting her or forcing her to leave the isle.

Was I even paying attention to the signs? I think, questioning how he could've fallen for someone, and I never even noticed. The reality of it is that I wasn't paying attention. Not really, at least. I was too stuck in my own misery and fake optimism to even notice that my oldest friend had fallen in love.

"You're right," she responds with a sniffle. She steps away to look him in the eye. "At least we can watch each other grow old. It'll just be with other people."

Seamus nods, and they stand there for a few long moments of silence. Just watching them breaks my heart. I had taken solace in the fact that neither Seamus nor I had anyone in our lives that we'd rather be with, but I was completely mistaken. How could I have been so blind? But even thinking such a thing, I know how.

I've been so selfish. Neither of us wanted this engagement, yet we let it happen all because our parents convinced us it was the best thing to do. The few times one of us spoke out, we were threatened into going along with it. Eventually, I focused on convincing myself that Seamus and I could be happy even if we didn't love each other. Never once did I imagine either one of us falling for someone else.

"Is this really the end?" Darina asks quietly.

"It has to be," Seamus says, and I can see the exhaustion and resignation on his face. "We both know we can't see each other again, especially after I get married. I won't hurt Cait. She hasn't done anything wrong to anyone in her entire life, and she doesn't deserve a husband who's in love with someone else."

His words are like a knife in my heart. Even in this pain and heartbreak, he's trying to do right by me. But what have I really done to deserve it? Aside from trying to please my parents and protect Enya from their schemes, I haven't done anything. We were forced into this engagement, both going along with it in the end. My mind spins as I try to think of anything I could've done to get our parents to see how terrible an idea this whole engagement really is, but nothing comes to mind.

What if I left? a small voice in the back of my head chimes in. *They can't force us to get married if one of us isn't here.*

"You're right," she responds with a small laugh, distracting me from my thoughts. "She's lucky to have you. You'll make a great husband, Seamus."

Not being able to hold back any longer, I step forward past the trees. A light pop in my head lets me know that I'm out of the barrier the Cailleach placed. Neither of them see me as they embrace once more. I can hear Darina's sobs, and while I can't hear Seamus's, his shaking shoulders as he cries silently are clear as day. I feel my own tears begin to fall, and I can't take it anymore.

"Why didn't you tell me?" I blurt out, breaking the air of sorrow. They both turn to me in shock. Seamus's face goes pale, and Darina starts crying even harder.

"I'm so sorry, Lady Caitria!" she exclaims as she falls to her knees. Seamus kneels next to her, trying to comfort her while searching for something to say as she cries uncontrollably, repeating her apologies. "I'm so sorry. Please believe me."

"We didn't mean for this to happen, Cait. I swear," Seamus says in a wavering voice, not meeting my eyes. "I'm so sorry. I promise I'll make it up to you for the rest of our lives."

I crouch down in front of Darina, wiping away my own tears without even looking at Seamus as he turns toward me. I can feel his eyes closely watching my every move, and his fear in this moment is palpable. I lightly touch her arm, and she cautiously turns her head up to look at me. She tries to control her sobs to little avail.

"Do you really love him?" I ask her softly. She's quiet as she searches my eyes for something. I can't tell what it is, but she seems to find it.

"So much," she quietly responds as tears continue streaming down her face. "I love him with my whole heart."

I nod at her answer and turn toward Seamus, who is still unable to look me in the eye.

"Seamus, why didn't you tell me?" I ask him.

"I'm so sorry," he says as his cheeks shine with tears. "I'd never do anything to hurt you, Cait. You have to know that."

"I know, but that doesn't answer my question," I tell him softly.

"You have to know that we never expected for this to happen," he says after a momentary pause. A few more tears escape and roll down his face as he continues. "We came here tonight to end things."

"I'm sorry," I mumble, and they both look at me with confusion.

"Aren't you upset?" Seamus asks, his disbelief clear on his face.

"Yes, but not for the reason you're thinking." I sigh as I sit down on the grass. "Let's sit and talk, yeah?"

Obediently, they both sit down to join me, purposefully keeping distance between them.

"So, how'd it happen?" I ask simply.

They share a look and remain silent. I sigh, understanding that they're hesitant to tell me anything. I don't blame them at all. If I were in their shoes, I'd be terrified to tell Seamus anything about my love life. He may be like my brother, but the engagement would certainly make me want to stay silent on the subject.

"I'm not upset about this," I say softly, not sure how best to explain myself. "I've been telling myself we'd be all right as long as were in this together. But I've been so wrapped up in my own head that I didn't even notice my best friend fell in love."

I wait for them to speak, but they remain silent. Picking a leaf off the ground, I twirl it between my fingers to have something to fidget with. I never imagined something like this would happen, but my own nervousness wasn't something I'd been prepared for. The looks on their faces and how they keep avoiding my eyes worries me.

At the very least, I hope Seamus will say something. For as long as I can remember, we talked about anything and everything. With the exception of my adventures in the forest, there's hardly ever been a secret between us. If he isn't willing to say anything, maybe it wasn't just him falling in love that I failed to notice, but also the crumbling of our friendship.

"Look, I love Seamus like a brother," I say after a few minutes of silence. "It's a horrible situation. This engagement wasn't our choice, and that hasn't changed. Marriage should be for love, and it should be celebrated." I pause and then sigh bitterly as a few stray tears escape my eyes. "*Your* love should be celebrated, and if I could do anything to make that a reality, I swear, I would."

I close my eyes to try and force back the tears when I feel a hand over mine. I look up and see Seamus comforting me, the tears in his own eyes threatening to escape. Even now, he's trying to make me feel better, and it just breaks me even more than I thought possible. It's cruel that someone who always puts others before himself won't even get a chance at being with who he loves.

"I just want you to be happy," I say, my voice barely going above a whisper as I feel a lump forming in my throat. "You deserve to be happy, Seamus."

"It was about two years ago, at O'Shaughnessy's pub," Seamus says quietly. "I saw her with a few of her mates. When she smiled, I felt like the wind had knocked me down."

"Really?" Darina asks as she looks over at him.

She's finally calmed down enough to where she is not completely sobbing, but a few tears still remain. She looks at him like he's the sun and the moon, and I can clearly see the love in her eyes.

"Took me a year to work up the courage to say hello," he says, a small smile creeping on his face as he looks down at his hands.

Even in the moonlight, I can see him blush. The way he looks at her is like she's the air he needs to breathe. They look at each other with such love and care, even as they're both clearly breaking, and that little voice chimes in again.

Seamus deserves this, it says. *They both do.*

"I'd only ever seen him at the pub, and when he came over to say hello that night, I felt like the luckiest girl alive," Darina adds quietly.

"After that…" Seamus clears his throat before slowly continuing, "She'd invite me to join her and her mates, and we just got to know each other. A few months after that, I'd asked if she wanted to meet up, just the two of us." He pauses as she reaches out to touch his hand, and he smiles at her with such love.

"We started to go on walks around her family's farm, and one day, she told me she loved me. That was a few months ago, and we've been meeting here a few times a week," he says and then immediately follows that up with one last thing. "I swear, Cait, nothing's happened other than talking. She knew we were engaged."

"We agreed that we'd just talk, especially with your engagement and all," Darina quickly adds. "We never wanted to do anything that might hurt you. Even talking felt wrong after a while. You don't deserve any of that."

I stay silent, nodding as I take in this information. They share a look, and Seamus opens his mouth to say something before hesitating. I stop fiddling with the leaf for a moment as more thoughts pop into my head.

What if I left the isle? I think. *Maybe then, they could be together. But how?*

"Cait," he says in a tentative tone. "Are you going to tell Lord and Lady Callihan about this? Or my parents?"

"What?" I say, sitting up straighter. "Seamus McNeillain, when have you ever known me to share secrets?" I look at both of them. "I swear that I won't tell anyone about this. I know better than anyone what the consequences would be if they found out about this."

Even just the thought of what might happen if anyone found out sends a shiver of fear down my spine. They both release a relieved sigh at me saying that.

"Thank you, Lady Caitria," Darina says softly, bowing her head in my direction.

"Please, call me Cait," I tell her with a smile as a laugh bubbles out. "Besides…" I look over at Seamus. He looks happier now than I have seen him in a very long time. "You've made Seamus very happy, and I'll be forever grateful for that."

"I can't tell you how relieved I am," Seamus says. "Thank you, Cait. Really, thank you."

"I wouldn't say that quite yet," I warn him. "Just because I'm happy for you both doesn't mean it can continue. You're right to worry. If our parents found out, I can't even imagine what would happen to Darina."

We sit in silence after that. There's no need for words to even consider what would happen to her. At the very least, our parents would make sure Darina would be blacklisted from finding a job. If they don't force her to marry someone in the village, they'd make her life so bad that she'd have to leave. And they wouldn't stop there. Her family would also be put in such a bad spot that they'd all need to leave the isle. Our parents learning about this could very likely mean the end of the Fitzpatrick family on Isle Draíocht.

"Lady Ca-Cait," Darina says after a moment. "How exactly did you find us?"

"I didn't even think of that," Seamus says with a suspicious tone in his voice. "How *did* you find us all the way out here?"

Before I can respond, two scraggly rabbits come bounding out of the trees. Darina lets out an audible gasp, and Seamus moves away at the sight of them. They both curl up and nestle themselves in my lap. The white one nudges my hand, a clear bid for attention, and I scratch its ear.

"Let's just say that I was drawn here," I tell them.

The three of us talk for a little while longer. Darina asks about the rabbit-like creatures, and Seamus warily tells her that they're harmless but doesn't go into details. He saw them a few times when we were children but always ran away whenever they approached me—something about their eyes scaring him.

They begin to open up after that. Darina shares stories about the amusing things Seamus would do during their visits to the forest, and Seamus points out things he'd seen her do on the few occasions they had met near the Fitzpatrick farm. I quietly watch them interact. Seeing their shared smiles and looks makes my heart ache for them.

In a way, they remind me of Shannon and Finn. They've always treated each other with so much love and kindness, and their happiness is infectious to those around them. An image pops into my mind of Seamus and Darina walking hand in hand around the village. The thought makes me smile, and I just know that, if given the chance, they'd love each other for their entire lives.

The pucai, listening to our conversations, remain nestled in my lap. I just listen and watch them interact until Darina stifles a yawn. I smile at her and stand up, realizing it's probably much later in the night than any of us expected.

"You know," I mention to Seamus as we're all getting ready to go our separate ways. "I don't see any reason why you two can't spend time together up to the wedding."

"Cait." He sighs as he looks across the clearing at Darina while she gets her bike unstuck from a particularly unruly bush. "We can't. You know that better than anyone."

"I know," I say, feeling frustrated at the situation on their behalf. "It's just not fair. Why shouldn't you be able to love who you want? Everyone should have that right."

"True," He agrees and gives me a sad smile. He nudges my shoulder with a tired acceptance in his eyes. "But I've come to terms with it. We both have." He sighs heavily. "We're getting married, and we may never love each other in that way, but we're in this together."

"Yeah, of course," I tell him with a forced smile. The grey puca nudges my leg with its nose and flicks its ear away from Seamus and Darina. "I'll see you later."

I give them both a hug before leaving, waving goodbye as I follow the pucai. They lag behind, taking a private moment to say goodbye to each other. Not even a moment later, I hear the creaking of a bicycle and know their final goodbyes are finished. My heart breaks for them as I think about how cruel this reality is.

Chapter 6

On my way out of the small clearing, the roots and plants move aside to form a path. The pucai hop ahead of me, and I follow them through the trees. It doesn't take long for me to realize they're leading me to the faerie tree in the deepest part of the forest. The will-o'wisps begin to show themselves, floating among the tree branches and bushes. Their short, quick movements look almost excited as they light up the path. Soon, they begin to illuminate a large, ancient tree.

"It has been a long time, young Caitria," a voice says, sounding as if it's coming from all around me.

The woman of the woods appears out of the darkness and gives me a warm smile. Her face is much older than it was when I last saw her, but the strength in the way she stands hasn't changed a bit.

"It's so good to see you, Lady Cailleach," I say, and I walk up to her.

I raise my arms, about to give her a hug when I freeze, realizing it would be very unwise to hug a faerie. She gives me a knowing smile as I drop my arms to my side. As a child, I wouldn't hesitate to throw myself into her arms, but now that I know who and what she is, I'm feeling a hint of fear. This is the first time in my life I've felt fear around them, and I don't like it.

"Sorcha, Glac, you did well," she says with a slight smile toward the pucai.

"It was an honor and a pleasure," the white one says as they both bow.

"So much time has passed, child," she says with a sigh before looking at me. "You're soon to be the ruler of the isle, are you not?"

"Yes, I guess I am," I tell her quietly as I look at the ground. Thinking about that future leaves a sour taste in my mouth. "Lady Cailleach, can I ask a question?"

"Of course," she says, and I can tell by the knowing look in her eyes that she already knows the answer.

"Why did you send the pucai to meet me tonight?" I ask.

"I can feel your sorrow, child," she says as she reaches out to lightly touch my cheek, not answering my question. The Cailleach gives me a small smile that doesn't reach her eyes as she continues. "You're connected to this land, Caitria. More so than other humans on the isle. Sorcha and Glac were drawn to you as a child, like they are with a number of children. But they remain so even though you have grown.

"This connection is not just with them, but with me as well, and others from our realm. It is also evident with the natural world near the Void." The Cailleach pauses for a moment, her smile fading before continuing on. "The trees and plants listen to you and have chosen to act on your behalf when necessary. This connection allows them to see your heart, and it also allows them to feel your pain."

"What? But why?" I ask, trying to wrap my mind around this. My heartbeat quickens, and I feel more confused than ever. I'd always thought that all of the strange things that happened were all the Cailleach's doing, but was it actually me? Does this mean I'm part faerie? Or am I something else entirely? My thoughts spiral as I think back.

At first, nothing comes to mind. Then I remember a conversation from earlier in the day. Cecilia said that I've always been able to pick the best berries and herbs from the garden. She's right, though. It was almost as if the best ones were on display, waiting to be picked. But that was always just luck. Wasn't it? It had to be. Just a skill I had picked up after spending so many hours outdoors as a child? But maybe not.

As soon as that hits me, a million little things begin to flood in. Every flower or plant I've ever walked past always looked like it stood up a little straighter. Any time I picked a flower, they always seemed to live a little longer. Whenever I would trip or fall, I almost always landed on a softer surface. When I fell earlier, I didn't land on the ground but on roots and moss that padded the ground.

Is it really such a surprise? I think after several other instances come to mind.

"What does that mean? How is that even possible?" I ask, trying to remain calm. "Am I even human?"

"You're as human as your ancestors," Cailleach simply says as she takes a step away from me. "This will all make sense one day. For now, it is time for you to leave, dear Caitria. Remember, you always have a choice."

"Wait!" I blurt out, wanting to stop her from leaving, but it's too late.

Just as quickly as she appeared, she vanished, taking away any chance I had at getting my questions answered. How could this all make sense? After everything I've witnessed tonight, nothing makes sense. In the span of a few hours, my entire world has just turned completely upside down. And what choice is she talking about? Is she talking about this strange connection I have with nature or something else entirely?

"It's time to return home," the white puca says, gently nudging my legs.

"Why did she leave so quickly?" I mumble, more to myself than anyone, as I turn and begin walking away from the tree. "What in the world was she talking about? What choice do I have? None of this makes any sense."

"The Lady Cailleach is always truthful. If she says it will make sense, it will," the grey puca says as it bumps me with its paw as we slowly walk.

"She can't remain in this world for long," The white puca says. "The veil is thinnest in the forest, but in her state, she's unable to traverse it for long."

"What do you mean, 'in her state'?" I ask, taking notice of the path being made for me with a newfound interest.

"Her time is coming to an end," the grey one explains. "She will be reborn when the moon goes dark."

"Reborn? As in she'll die and come back to life?" I ask, even more confused at what the puca just said.

"Yes," the grey puca says simply.

"Her life is like the seasons," the white one adds. "She always dies this time of year, but she'll come back with the first light of the moon."

My mind spins at this new piece of information. However, something tells me now isn't the time to dwell on that. "What did she mean when she said I have a choice? What choice?"

"Perhaps it's exactly that," the white puca replies. "You have a choice."

"But what choice do I have? What was she even talking about?" I ask with a frustrated sigh.

"You do not wish to be married, yes? Perhaps you can either do what you are told to do or do something else," the grey puca says after a moment.

We walk most of the way back in silence. I glance up at the will-o'-wisps and notice that they do, in fact, appear to follow me a little. Their gentle blue light illuminates the part of the way back before they begin to return to the tree.

"You may use our names," the white puca says as we get to the edge of the forest, pulling me back from my thoughts.

"What?" I ask, not quite sure I heard right.

After everything that's happened tonight, I didn't think I could feel any more shocked. Even though I know very little about the world of the fae, one thing I do know from all the stories and myths I've heard is that a faerie's name is something humans shouldn't say unless they have permission. It's a powerful thing, so the puca's statement takes me by surprise.

"I am Glac," the grey puca says before looking toward the white puca sitting next to it. "And this is Sorcha."

"Oh," I say, feeling a wave of emotion overtake me. For some reason, this feels like a final goodbye. I crouch down as they sit up on their back legs so we can be at eye-level. "Glac, Sorcha, thank you so much for guiding me safely."

They lean into me, and I give them a hug as a few tears escape from my eyes. I sniffle as I hold them for a moment. Their soft fur is a comforting reminder of the past.

"You were my favorite child," Sorcha says as we break away from one another.

"Please call upon us whenever you need us, Lady Caitria," Glac says before they both hop into the forest, disappearing from sight.

I wave into the darkness before making my way down the hill and back to the manor. After quietly sneaking back inside, making sure to be as silent as possible, I lie down in bed. It'll be an early morning, but no matter how hard I try, I'm simply unable to fall asleep.

Perhaps I just don't show up to the wedding, I think, reminded of my thoughts earlier. *What would happen then?*

It's a crazy thought. I've known since I was thirteen that Seamus and I would be engaged. Our parents left little room for discussion when they sat us down in Father's study that fateful morning. It was hard to process why they wanted this, but as we got older, the reason became clear—power.

One of us needs to disappear, I think. *That's the only way to stop the wedding. But is it even possible?*

Chapter 7

I wake up the next morning with a sharp knock at my door. Not wanting to deal with the angry face I know is waiting for me on the other side of the door, I quickly run into the bathroom and turn on the water for the shower.

"Caitria, are you still bathing?" Mother's exasperated voice is accompanied by the slamming of my bedroom door. "How many times must I tell you? You are expected to be prepared every day in case someone should request your presence. If you are not ready to see me and your father off in the next ten minutes, there will be hell to pay!" she shrieks. The sound of her voice sends a wave of anxiety that has my stomach in knots. I wash my hair, making sure to get out any and all dirt or twigs that may have been stuck in it from my outing last night.

I can practically see the anger on her face as I close my eyes to prevent any soap from getting into them. Mother, with her tightly done hair and permanent scowl lines that have formed over the last several years, must be bright red. The loud clacking of her low heels is followed by the slamming of my bedroom door.

Knowing she's likely gone down the stairs to see Father, I make quick work of drying off and throwing on some simple makeup. It's never a good sign when she gets Father involved. His indifference to my actions only fuels her anger, usually turning it into a rage. After wringing my hair to get as much water out as I can, I throw on a simple blue long-sleeved dress and a pair of low-heeled Oxfords before going downstairs.

"You're late!" Mother exclaims, the red flush on her skin a clear indicator that she's more on-edge than usual this morning. "Ernest, look at your child. She is an absolute disgrace to the Callihan name. What will everyone think?"

"It's not as if she'll be leaving the manor, Agatha," Father says. He gives me a nod of acknowledgment before turning away from me. "The only ones that will see her this morning are the help, and why should we care what they think of her?"

"Because people talk, Ernest," Mother seethes as she wraps a thick green shawl around her shoulders. "What if someone says something?"

"No one will talk," Father scolds her. "They know that talking will cost them their livelihood. And it isn't as if Caitria will be behaving this way later today."

Mother looks like she wants to say something else but only purses her lips and storms out of the manor and toward the car where Alan is waiting.

"You need to grow up and realize that such childish behavior will not be tolerated," Father says to me in a low, calm voice as he puts on his coat. "You are the future lady of Draíocht, and I expect you to act like it. Whether you like it or not, you *will* be the future leader of this land. This behavior will cease now, and if I hear anything bad from your outing later this evening, the consequences will be dire. Do you understand me?"

"Yes, Father. My apologies," I respond, not able to look him in the eyes when he's this angry.

While Father isn't usually a violent man, his words are sharper than any sword. His threats don't fall on deaf ears, either. The one and only time he raised a hand to me was immediately after I protested the forced engagement. Afterward, I wasn't allowed to sleep for three days, and every single one of the books and plants I had been previously allowed to keep in my room were removed and destroyed.

"See to it that this never happens again, and your apologies might finally mean something," he seethes right before he heads out to the car where Mother is waiting, slamming the front door behind him.

I flinch at the sound and stand there for a moment to calm myself. The tears that begin to form in my eyes won't disappear no matter how many times I try to blink them away. Their words sting, even after hearing them for so many years. How could they ever treat someone this way, let alone their own child?

"Cait?" I hear a soft voice say from behind me. It instantly pulls me away from my own thoughts. Discreetly wiping away the tears, I turn around to find Enya hiding in the shadows of the staircase. "Are you all right?"

"Of course, Enya," I say, forcing a smile. "Why?"

"I'm not a little girl anymore, Cait," she says as she takes a few steps toward me. "You don't have to hide it from me."

"I'm not hiding anything," I tell her with a smile.

Pulling her in for a hug, I quickly blink away the tears that continue to form. Her arms wrap around my waist. It's so warm and comforting that I don't want to let go. If only I could protect her from everything, I would do it in a heartbeat. However, I can only do so much. I take a deep breath before pulling away, giving her a bright, well-rehearsed smile.

"I have studying to do, but perhaps we can have lunch together?" I say hopefully.

"All right," she replies with a small wave as I walk out toward the library. "I'll be in the kitchen if you need me."

Walking down the hallway to the back corner of the manor, I open the heavy wooden door to the small library. The door shuts behind me with an audible thud, and I take a deep breath as silence falls around me. While I feel most comfortable surrounded by nature, something about the wooden shelves, the smell of paper, and the fireplace of the library also bring me comfort.

The sunlight streaming in through the curtains that have been left cracked open mingles with the dust in the air, giving the entire room a hazy glow. In a way, it feels almost magical. I walk over to the nearest bookshelf and brush my fingers along their spines as I read the titles. This room holds a way for someone to travel the world from the comfort of the couch or to be transported back to a time when magic was once widely found on the isle. It also holds books on every topic imaginable—from history to politics. I distinctly remember struggling through the law books last year. Being the next lady of Draíocht, this room that I once loved became a place of boredom, frustration, and in some instances, a place I feared to go.

As a child, there were even a few rare occasions where Mother would read Enya and me books about all the myths and legends of our land. It was always warm and cozy as we all curled up on the couch by the fire. That, however, was years ago. As I stand here, looking around the room, I realize just how little it's changed over the years.

The shelves stand tall along the four walls of the room, and with the exception of the gap for the fireplace and a painting of the first queen of Isle Draíocht hanging above it, it's completely filled with books. Two roller ladders lean against one of the walls, the track along the ceiling allowing for quick and easy movement to either side of the room. The floor-to-ceiling bookshelves that divide the back half of the room in two are more recent additions, but they look as though they have always been there. The well-loved couch in front of the fireplace is bookended by two side tables, which have been known to hold the spare book waiting to be returned to its home as well as hundreds of tea cups and other beverages depending on the time of day.

Focusing on the task at hand, I think back to the book of fairy-tales Mother used to read from. I quickly find it and pull it from the shelf. The leather-bound book is soft and worn with time. The tree of life decorates the cover, its roots and branches intertwined. It has no title, though none is really needed. The tree is only ever used in documents with the myths and legends of faeries. I take a seat on the couch, curling my legs under me, and crack open the book.

The first pages it opens to are illustrations of various creatures. Flipping past the colorful images of leprechauns, merrows, will-o'wisps, and banshees, I stop on the section about the Cailleach. To see her image, especially in this book, feels so strange.

I read through the various stories about the old hag known to roam the forests of Isle Draíocht. Parents told their kids stories like hers to scare them into staying away from the trees, especially after dark, when she was rumored to have more power. She was told to have the power over shadows and all sorts of other spooky things that roam freely at night. As I continue reading, I feel my eyes get heavy. The consequences of staying out so late immediately make themselves known as my eyes drift closed.

After what feels like just minutes, I abruptly wake up from the sound of the crackling fire. Feeling panicked at the sound, I immediately jump off the couch, looking around the room. I let out a sigh of relief as I realize the fire is well-contained in the fireplace, and the metal curtain is closed to prevent any embers from jumping out. Taking a deep breath, I allow myself a moment of peace as I watch the fire burn, feeling the warmth on my skin.

Looking toward the window at the far end of the wall, I'm shocked to see the sun, which was high in the sky when I entered the library, is now long gone, having been replaced by the moon. I stand up when I hear the sound of someone sipping a beverage from somewhere at the far end of the room. I look toward the bookshelves and brace myself for whatever is waiting for me as I hear footsteps coming closer.

Mother would be absolutely furious if she found me asleep. While she usually spends her evenings in the sitting room just off the side of Father's office, she has invited Maureen Hadden and Brigit McNeillain over for a cup of tea in the library in the past. As fellow ladies of the isle, she always strives to maintain her image of friendliness just in case one of them decides to try and isolate her. I mentally brace myself for her disappointment and the slap that I'm undoubtedly about to receive as the sound of footsteps gets closer and closer. However, when a figure emerges from the shadows, I am shocked to see someone else standing there.

The Cailleach has never once entered the manor. At least, I've never heard of her visiting here before. However, she looks just as comfortable here as she does in the forest. Holding a teacup, she gives me a warm, knowing smile before moving to the couch.

"I may not have much love for these human structures, but this is my land," Cailleach tells me in a calm, serene voice as she takes a seat.

I glance at her, unable to focus on her facial features for long before they shift. One moment, she looks like she could be my age, and the next, she is as old as time itself. Other times, she looks as though she could be the same age as Mother. Her hair remains a silvery color, which nicely complements her moss-green dress.

"You have begun to make your choice," she says simply.

"Is there really a choice?" I ask her as I take a seat.

"Yes," the Cailleach replies with a serious look. "The path will be difficult, but it is still one you can take."

She waves her hand slightly and, in the blink of an eye, a cup appears floating in front of me. It's a shock to see her use magic, but I try to maintain my composure. I carefully take it from the air, immediately wary. Not wanting to be rude but also not wanting to fall for any tricks, I attempt to inspect its contents without her noticing. While she's never given me a reason to be suspicious, I've read my fair share of stories about faeries who lure young people into the Otherworld using a variety of means, food being one of them.

"Worry not, young Caitria," she says with an amused look. "It is brambleberry tea, made from plants you humans use."

"Thank you," I quietly say as I take a sip. It is pleasantly both sweet and tart, with a slight hint of something herbal.

"You are leaving, then?" she asks, though it sounds more like she is making a statement. I see a look of sad acceptance in her face as she says this.

"I'm going to try," I reply quietly. "It's the only way."

"So it seems," Cailleach responds simply. Bringing her cup to her mouth, she takes a sip of tea before speaking. "Tell me, Caitria, why do you think I allow you to see me, even as you grow?"

While confused at her question, I think on this for a minute, knowing it can't be a simple answer. There are probably many reasons why she allowed me to see her when I was younger. A lot of children on the isle have claimed to see her. However, most people who see her eventually blame it on their imagination, just like I did. So why can I still see her?

It can't be because I'm the future lady of Draíocht. If that were the case, Mother would've been able to see her. It must not be just because of my love of nature. I'm not the only one who isn't afraid to spend time in the forest.

After giving myself a minute to think, something comes to mind. I hesitate before replying, "Is it because of what you mentioned last night?"

"In part, yes," Cailleach begins as she sits back on the couch, making herself comfortable. "Allow me to share a story."

I nod quietly, curious about what she'll share. She takes a sip of her tea before she begins.

"Many years ago, I was walking through the forest, as I have since before your people called this land home. This day, I encountered something I had not seen before. Sorcha and Glac were playing with a human. As you know, faeries will rarely interact with your kind for anything longer than a few fleeting moments. While harmless, they tend to avoid humans to ensure their safety. However, here were two pucai, playing with a child. Only after watching their interactions did I notice the child had a strange aura."

I silently listen as she tells her story. As she talks, I can practically see what she's talking about, almost as if I'm right there. I can smell the clean air and feel the light breeze on my skin. I close my eyes, and in that brief second, I've been transported to the forest behind the manor. The sound of a child's laughter fills the air, and I see the pucai playing with a young girl in a brown linen dress. A soft yellow light surrounds her as they play.

"I returned to my realm and asked the elders what it meant," Cailleach continues, her voice sounding no louder than a whisper as I watch the scene before me change. "They were confused by this as well. After consulting the old texts, they found that this human was born with the gift of Sight."

A question bubbles up inside my mind, but I push it aside, knowing I shouldn't interrupt her. In front of me, the atmosphere shifts as the pucai stop playing with the child. She grows into a young woman in an instant, the light around her growing stronger.

"This gift allows them to sense when those from the Otherworld are nearby. They can interact with us without being persuaded and are able to cross the veil, the gateway between our realms, by themselves. This child had a particularly strong Sight, and she was able to manipulate the world around her." She takes another sip of tea before she continues.

Before me, the young woman raises an arm, gently swaying it back and forth as the trees and plants around her mimic her movements. It's a wondrous sight, identical to what I witnessed as a child. Soon the image fades.

"The more we learned, the more dangerous I realized humans with Sight are. In the past, many children were born with the gift." She sighs, and I feel a chill go down my spine.

The sound of a crying baby pierces the air as the world around me shifts, the image illuminated by the moon above. I'm standing over an old wooden cradle, watching as a small creature takes the crying child, replacing it with a silent one. I reach out to stop them, but the image evaporates, almost as if it's being blown away in the wind.

"We exchanged those children for nongifted faeries. I believe your people called them Changelings. We would bring them to places near a Void, a protective barrier, where we could watch them. Once the human was no longer a threat, we would give them back," she tells me.

The pieces of her story are beginning to come together, and I feel sick at the implications. I see that same scene take place over and over. Each time, I'm unable to stop the child from being switched. Their cries echo in my ears as I try to save them. It isn't until I watch the tenth child get taken that I realize something. Every single stolen child was surrounded by a faint yellow light.

"We stopped such things a few hundred years ago when we realized that most children born near a Void have the gift to some extent. We began to observe and learned that all humans lose this gift before they reach their fifth year of life. The elders and I decided we would only monitor those with Sight to ensure they would not become a threat." After another pause for tea, Cailleach continues with the story.

I watch before me as a group of children play in the forest, accompanied by a soft breeze and the sunlight shining down through the trees. The tell-tale glow of the puca's golden eyes can be seen in the bushes as they watch. In just a few seconds, the children age several years. The yellow glow around them fades as they age until, eventually, it's completely gone.

"Time passed after that first child. Centuries went by, and I eventually tasked the pucai to your world. Their kind are easily able to see such things and are very loyal. They would notify me if they came across a child with a strong gift of Sight," she says before pausing.

The images around me fade once again, morphing into the library. It's a jarring shift, and I'm in shock by everything I just saw. After a glance at my tea cup, Cailleach waves her hand, and both cups refill with hot tea.

"With time, veils around the world went dormant until only a few remained," Cailleach says after a sip. "The elders requested I place a Void to protect the remaining veils." She pauses for a bit longer than normal, and I see something in her that I haven't really ever seen before.

As she looks up at the painting of the first queen of Draíocht, a loving smile forms on her face, much like Shannon's, whenever she looks at Cecilia. The room around us changes, and suddenly, a little girl is sitting on the ground in front us.

"A few centuries ago, a child was born. The pucai notified me of the strength of the child's gift," she tells me, looking over at me. "I crossed the Void to see her. She was kind and strong willed, and even in one so young, I could tell this child was destined for great things." She pauses and looks down at the tea in her hands.

The child in front of us is playing with rocks, her wild hair moving softly moving in the breeze. The pucai hop around her, bringing her all sorts of little leaves and twigs. The glow surrounding her is almost blinding every time she touches them. Her giggling intensifies as one twig in her hand begins to lengthen and sprout leaves.

"I decided to watch her myself." She takes a deep breath before continuing, looking down at the little girl as the image fades away, and we're once again in the library.

"Over time, we bonded and she became like a daughter to me. When invaders threatened this land, thinking it was full of long-lost magic, I gifted the young woman the ability to protect her people. She was able to bring together the three clans that resided here, and they combined forces and protected the isle."

The story she tells is one I've heard many times before. The story of the first Caitria is the story of my people. She saw invaders were coming from the mainland early one evening. Throughout the night, she worked to bring the clan leaders together to fight to protect our people. While the clans had never been openly hostile toward one another, they had no trust among them. At barely nineteen years old, she succeeded in bringing them together.

She herself was on the front lines when the invaders arrived. An excellent strategist, her quick thinking and foresight resulted in no lives lost from any of the three clans. Some say her words forced the invaders to leave and never return, and others say she killed their leader before they could even leave their boats. Regardless of what actually happened, the clans all agreed that she should be queen of Draíocht.

"After their victory, the people crowned her their queen. She reigned for a number of years before granting the clan leaders similar power. You see, as she aged, she would come to me with offerings of thanks and for counsel. In doing so, she realized that the best thing for her people was to have not one leader, but several." Cailleach looks down and stays quiet for a moment.

Before I realize it, I reach out to place a hand over hers to provide some comfort. She freezes for a moment before looking up at me. I see a look of thanks in her eyes. The Cailleach does not pull her hand away but squeezes mine before I pull away.

"It was one of her final acts before passing," she tells me. We sit in silence for a moment. I don't even have to look over to know that the Cailleach is lost in her memories.

"Then," she adds. "Not long ago, I received word from the pucai that another human was born with a Sight that was comparable with the previous child. When I arrived, I found you. I was curious to see what kind of human you would be and hid in the shadows so I would remain out of sight. But you sensed me. Even as a young child, it was clear that your gift is just as strong as your ancestor's."

"But what does that mean?" I ask, trying to wrap my head around this information. "Why do I still have the Sight?"

"You share many similarities with her, not just her gift," Cailleach replies with a warmth in her eyes.

"Is that why you told me I have a choice?" I ask quietly. "Because of her?"

"Yes, it is," Cailleach says. "Your ancestor, from whom you take your name, caused a great change in the people of this land. You will make a change in the people here too. Of that, I am certain."

"But how?" I ask, feeling very lost. "No matter what I do, they never listen."

"You're right, young Caitria," she says, "but you underestimate yourself. You are stronger than you think, and your actions create more change than you can ever know."

"It doesn't feel that way," I mumble when suddenly a question comes to me. "Did you know I would decide to leave?"

"Yes," she says after a moment.

"Where am I supposed to go? What happens after I leave?" I ask, hoping the Cailleach might know more than she's letting on.

"Trust your instincts, Caitria," Cailleach tells me cryptically. "You will know where you're meant to be."

The room around me grows hazy, and I can tell something isn't right. I look around to see the room begin to go dark, the shadows inching closer with every second that passes.

"I have been here too long," I hear Cailleach say as I feel something warm in my palm. "You will need this."

I can no longer see her as the world goes black, and I feel myself falling.

Chapter 8

I shoot up, gasping as I feel a rush of air flowing into my lungs. I look around the room and realize the sun is shining outside, streaming through the curtains that are partially cracked. The fireplace, which had been crackling with life only moments ago, is now completely void of any sign that it had been lit. Any sign of the tea cups and brambleberry tea is long gone.

I'm about to dismiss everything that just happened to an over-active imagination when I realize something is in my right hand. Opening it slowly, I see a small silver pendant on a thin, delicate chain. It looks familiar with its delicate and intricate silver strands woven into a knot, though I have a hard time placing it.

I know I must be crazy to think what happened was even remotely real, but it must've been. Looking around the room, and it's clear no one has come in or out of the library. Everything looks exactly the same as when I came in. How else would this end up in my hand if that strange dream wasn't real?

I slip the necklace over my head and hide it under my blouse before putting away the book of fairytales. As I walk back to the fireplace, I pause and look up at the painting of the first queen of Draíocht. Queen Caitria, my namesake, looks down at me with the same nose and eyes that I see every day. A delicate silver crown sits on her wild brown hair. It's strange to think someone who was barely older than I am once commanded such power and respect.

I wonder for a moment what, exactly, the Cailleach gave her. It must've been some sort of weapon if she was able to use it to protect her people. However, she was also known to avoid bloodshed whenever possible, so a weapon doesn't make much sense. Whatever it was, it never was mentioned in the history books.

I'm about to turn away when something catches my eye. Squinting up at the painting once more, I notice something hiding beneath a layer of dust. I quickly pull over one of the step stools from a shelf nearby and climb up. Carefully using my sleeve to brush away years of dust and grime from the paint, my breath catches in my throat at what I see. The detail is so small that I'd never noticed it before. However, there it is, clear as day. Hanging around her neck on a thin chain is a small, silver pendant in the shape of a knot.

I touch it and wonder if this was the gift Cailleach had given to Queen Caitria. She said I'd need it but gave me no instructions on what it does or how it works. My mind begins to spin at the possibilities of what it could do. It doesn't look like a weapon, so perhaps it does something else?

Perhaps I'll know how to use it when I need it, I think. When I'll need it, though, I've no idea.

A knock on the library door draws me from my thoughts. The door opens as Alan steps past the threshold and gives me a slight bow.

"May I suggest some lunch, Lady Caitria?" he asks in a calm voice.

"Of course," I say as my stomach growls in agreement.

"Very good," he tells me with a kind smile as we walk down the hallway. "I believe Lady Enya has been helping Miss Shannon since this morning."

"Oh, wonderful," I say as I get closer to the kitchen. "Do you know what they've been making?"

"Cait," a voice exclaims as we arrive. "I'm so happy you came to join us."

Enya rushes over to me with a wide smile. She gives me a quick hug before ushering me to a stool, leaving little room for protest. Her joy is almost infectious, and I feel my spirits lift a little.

"Miss Shannon has been teaching me all sorts of things, and you're just in time to try some," Enya tells me excitedly.

"Let me put the kettle on," Shannon says with a smile as she busies herself, filling the kettle with water before setting it up on one of the hot burners on the stove.

I take a seat on one of the stools at the large kitchen island and quietly watch as they busy themselves. As Enya takes things off cooling racks at the opposite end of the counter, Shannon places three mugs in front of me. She drops the metal steepers in as the water begins to boil. I watch as she fills each mug, feeling a strange sense of calm as the tea leaves create a wave of color in the water.

"I saw the most curious thing this morning," Shannon quietly remarks as she uses a spoon to stir in a lump of sugar and removes the now steeped tea leaves.

"What was that?" I ask as she pours a dash of milk in the mug.

"When I came in this morning, I saw tracks of dirt coming in from the garden. I thought the pucai had snuck in during the night," she tells me with a light laugh, making sure to keep her voice low enough that only I can hear her.

I feel the blood drain from my face and force myself to remain as calm as I possibly can. Mother and Father have used people working around the manor as informants before. Mother left a particularly nasty bruise on my arm after a house cleaner saw me walking around the kitchen garden without her permission. Shannon and Alan are the only two who've never said anything to get me in trouble, but I'm always on edge whenever they see something they shouldn't.

"It's all cleaned up now, but I've half a mind to let those pesky goblins know that the broom by the door can be used to clean up their own mess," Shannon tells me with a pointed look.

"Is that so?" I say with a nervous laugh stuck in my throat. "Well, I'm sure that if you leave them a note, they'll get the message."

"Perhaps I'll do just that," she replies and gives me a small smile, passing a mug into my hands. "Still, they must've had a grand old time. While I could do without the dirt in my kitchen, I hope they continue to come to visit."

I give her a smile in response as I let out a sigh of relief. Enya brings a platter over as I take a sip from the steaming mug. It's covered in a towel, and Shannon chuckles at the sight. I feel tears threaten to form in my eyes as I see her joy and excitement. To think that this is one of the things I'll be leaving behind makes my heart ache, but I know it'll all be worth it. As long as I do things right, she'll never have to go through what I have.

"Are you ready to see the fruits of our labor?" Enya asks excitedly before removing the towel with a flourish.

The platter is completely filled with bread, scones, a variety of jams, butter, and honey. She's sliced the barmbrack, and there's even smoked fish and boxty. A few of Shannon's honey shortbread biscuits also make an appearance. It really is a mini feast.

"You really went all-out," I tell them both as my stomach growls loudly. "This looks delicious."

"Oh, this was all Lady Enya," Shannon says as she takes a seat next to me. "I was merely here to assist."

"Enya, you really did all this?" I ask in awe.

Enya nods shyly in response, and I stand up, pulling her in and hugging her tightly.

"This is amazing, and I'm so proud of you."

"Thanks, Cait," she mumbles into my shoulder as she squeezes me in response. "Miss Shannon's been teaching me how to make all sorts of things."

"Why are you learning to cook?" I ask her out of curiosity as we each take a seat at the counter.

"No reason, really," she mumbles as she passes us napkins and plates. The color blooming in her cheeks tells a very different story.

"Me thinks a young man has caught her fancy," Shannon sings lightly, placing a thick slice of bread on my plate.

Enya's face grows even more red as she opens her mouth to protest.

"Well, I mean, you know," she mumbles, unable to get her words together.

"Is that true?" I ask, slightly upset that she never told me.

I can't really blame her, though. She hasn't had much of a chance to tell me anything lately. One of us is usually busy doing something, and that one is typically me. It certainly doesn't help that Mother and Father rarely involve her in anything, and I'm usually too busy to spend much time with her, if any.

"I wouldn't say it's not untrue," Enya says as she tries to avoid my eyes. She takes a moment to search for the words and eventually, she sighs. "I mean, your birthday is tomorrow too, and I wanted to make you a cake, but then I remembered how much you loved barmbrack when we visited the mainland."

"I completely forgot," I mumble to myself before taking a bite of the delicious fruity bread. The wedding had taken over my mind to the point that I completely forgot that my own birthday is tomorrow. "And I can't believe you remembered that. You weren't even six years old when we went to the mainland."

"Of course I remember," Enya says softly, and I notice a few tears forming in her eyes. "That's the only trip we ever took as a family. How could I forget it?"

I place a hand over one of hers as she wipes her tears with her free hand. She gives me a watery smile and looks down. For a moment, I can really see the young woman she's becoming. The pain in her eyes is clear, but so is the love in her voice. My heart breaks once again as I realize just how much I'm giving up by leaving.

They'll all gain so much, though, I tell myself.

"Now," I say, clearing my throat as we begin putting more food on our plates, "tell me about this boy."

"He's really kind, and he has nice eyes," Enya says as a blush once again creeps into her cheeks.

"What's his name?" I ask. "Do I know him?"

"Of course you know him, Cait," Enya says with a little eye roll. "Between all the festivals and holidays, you meet everyone on Isle Draíocht at least once a year."

"You're not wrong about that, but what's his name?" I ask with a smile. It's a refreshing change to talk about someone else, especially as it's also letting me spend a nice time with Enya and Shannon.

"William," Enya says softly after a second.

When I hear the name, the hazy image of a young man with wavy black hair comes to mind. "His father is the carpenter in town. Right?" I ask, straining my memory to fill in the gaps.

"His dad made the most beautiful table for me and Finn a few years ago!" Shannon gushes right before taking a bite of a slice of barmbrack smothered in butter and honey. "And his mum is an excellent cook. Very traditional stuff. She's the one who makes all the traditional Irish food for our celebrations."

"I remember him now. He seemed really lovely," I tell her as the face in my mind grows clearer, and Enya blushes in response. "He does have a beautiful smile."

"I really do like him, Cait," she says after a moment. "Miss Shannon always says that the way to a man's heart is his stomach. I'm not sure if I'd ever be able to make him anything that lives up to his mum's, but I hoped that if I started learning, maybe it'll happen."

"I'm sure he'll love whatever you make," I assure her. "Have you told him how you feel?"

"I want to, but I'm scared," she says with a look of defeat on her face as she looks down at her hands, fidgeting with a loose string on her sweater. "What if he doesn't like me back? Or what if he does? What would we do? Mother and Father wouldn't ever approve."

"If you could be together, would you tell him?" I ask, thinking I might possibly be able to help with that.

"I'd hope so!" Shannon says. "Lady Enya's been visiting me for ages by now for cooking lessons. She deserves to know that her efforts were worthwhile."

"But what if I tell him and he laughs in my face," Enya whispers as the color drains from her face. "I'd never be able to show my face in town again."

"You'll be able to because he won't say no," I tell her. "If I remember right, he couldn't take his eyes off you during Samhain last month. I'd be willing to bet that he's just as nervous as you and likes you just as much."

"Really?" Enya whispers with a look of hope in her eyes.

"Really," I tell her as I give her a hug. She pulls away a moment later with yet another sigh.

"Do you think he'll be at the pub tonight?" she asks me.

"Oh, he'll be there," Shannon assures her. "Lord and Lady Callihan made sure everyone knows about the engagement party tonight. Everyone in town's been excited about it for months now. Besides, it's not every day one of our future leaders gets married."

"Mother and Father probably won't attend," I add, giving Enya a pointed look. "It'd be the perfect opportunity to tell him how you feel."

"They won't, but their spies will," Enya exclaims in frustration. "I'd never be able to walk over to him without them finding out. Not in a million years. Especially since this is the first time in months that they've agreed to let me go into town."

"True," I relent. "But I've got a feeling they'll be paying closer attention to me."

"Are you sure?" she asks, and I can see the hope hiding in her eyes.

"I'm positive," I tell her, placing a hand over hers and giving it a light squeeze. "Mother and Father will want to know everything I do to make sure I don't do anything unbecoming."

"You're positive they won't find out?" Enya asks again after a moment. "I don't want to ask myself 'what if' for the rest of my life, but I also don't want you to get in trouble."

"Don't you worry about that," I tell her, patting her hand. "I won't get in trouble, and neither will you."

"And you're sure Gerald won't say anything to his parents?" Enya asks, sounding a little more hopeful.

Only child of the Hadden clan, Gerald has never been someone to spy for any of our parents. He knows just how terrible it can be to have them breathing down our necks, wanting to know every single little detail about our lives. His own parents aren't much better, and he's always made a point to act however he pleases. Thankfully for us, he just so happens to be fiercely protective of his friends. Spying on Enya would be the last thing he'd do.

"I highly doubt he'd say anything," I tell her. "His parents would definitely want to know, but Gerald Hadden isn't the kind of person to see and tell."

"You're right," Enya says with a relieved sigh.

"It's settled then," I reply, a smile slowly forming on my face. "You'll tell him tonight."

Chapter 9

After lunch, I head up to my room to start getting ready for the engagement party. Over a week ago, Mother and Brigit invaded my closet to find the perfect thing for me to wear. While I'd wanted to pick my own clothes just this once, I feel a small bit of excitement knowing that this might be one of the last times I'm forced to wear something.

I head to the bathroom and make sure I'm properly groomed and cleaned before meticulously applying a thin layer of makeup on my face. Mother and Brigit picked out a long-sleeve, light green dress that brushes my calves, and a pair of simple black heels. While it's not what I would've chosen, I know this is a battle I'd never win. I slip into the dress and am about to zip it up when I hear a knock at the door.

"Come in," I say, recognizing Enya's knock.

She comes in pushing a meal cart, only to get it caught on the edge of the doorframe. I hurry over to catch the door before it falls closed. Enya gives me an embarrassed smile as she pushes the cart the rest of the way into the room.

"I thought we could have some tea?" she asks as she looks down at her hands. I look at the cart and see a steaming teapot with two cups. There's also a plate of biscuits and a small cup of the milk.

"I'd love to," I tell her with a smile as I pull two chairs together. We both move the cart to the chairs so we can enjoy our tea more comfortably. "You look beautiful, by the way."

"Oh, thanks, Cait," she replies as she pours us each a cuppa. Her dark blue dress and simple flats make her look older than her fourteen years. They nicely complement her pale skin and dark hair.

"I can't remember the last time we shared a cup of tea like this," I say, more to myself than anyone, as I recall those nights.

"I know," Enya says wistfully, looking down at the cup in her hands. "I was thinking about it at lunch. You get married in two days. We won't be able to do this after you're married, so I thought, why not do it one last time."

"Oh, Enya," I say as I lean over and give her a hug.

The tears form in her eyes and begin to fall before I can do anything. All too soon, she's sobbing. Little does she know, this will indeed be the last time we have tea together for a long time, but not for the reason she thinks. My heart breaks at the sound of her crying, but I know better than to try and get her to stop. Sometimes, all you really need is to just let it out.

"No matter what, we'll always be sisters," I tell her after a few minutes. "Nothing's going to change that."

"I know." She sniffles in a small voice before she sobs once again. "But everything'll be different."

"Talk to me, Enya," I beg. Enya has always been cheerful, and seeing her crying so much puts me on edge. "What's going on?"

"It's nothing. I promise," she says as she looks at me with watery eyes. Her mouth trembles as she buries her head in my shoulder.

"It doesn't seem like nothing," I tell her as I stroke her hair like I used to when we were little.

"It just feels like everything's going by so fast," Enya tells me with a sniffle as she breaks away from our hug. "You know, I've always wanted to see you in your wedding dress. You'd think, being your sister and all, Mother would've made an exception just this once and let me come with you," She sniffles and wipes away a few tears. "You'll be busy being married and having babies. I guess I'm just scared that you won't have time for me anymore."

"That'll never happen," I tell her in a soft yet firm voice. "I'll never not have time for you."

"You promise?" she asks me through her tears as a small smile forms on her face.

"I promise," I tell her as I smile in response. "And if I ever don't have time, I'll make time."

"Well, good," Enya says as she forces a smile. "I'm sorry."

"What're you sorry for?" I ask her as I grab her a napkin from the cart to wipe off her tears.

"I wanted us to have a fun tea time, but all I've done so far is get tears all over your dress," she tells me as she wipes her eyes.

"Don't worry about that at all," I say, waving away her concerns. "Tears will do absolutely nothing to it. It'll dry before you know it."

"Okay," she tells me.

After a brief sniffle, she calms down a little before taking a biscuit from the cart and biting into it. I lean back in my chair and watch her quietly. I blink away tears that threaten to form. If I leave, what'll happen to Enya? Mother and Father have all but ignored her since she was ten years old. Sure, it's saved her from everything I've experienced, but at what cost? Even behind her sunshine exterior, I know she's scared. She deserves to be loved and cared for, something she should've gotten from our parents.

If all goes to plan, she'll never go through what I went through, I think. *And she'll be loved and safe.*

"Cait, can I ask a question?" she asks, pulling me from my thoughts.

"You know you can ask me anything," I reply after taking a sip of my tea.

"What does love feel like?" Enya softly asks as she looks at her fidgeting hands.

"What?" I respond, not entirely sure if I heard her right.

A pang of guilt shoots through me. We were sworn to secrecy on the arranged marriage. The only people who know are me, Seamus, and our parents. The entire reason they wanted us to get married in the first place is because it'd consolidate their power and because it'd be believable with our close friendship. Enya wasn't ever supposed to know.

Should I tell her the truth? I wonder. She deserves to know, but maybe it's better that she doesn't know right now. In a split second, I make the decision to let her know after the pub tonight.

"You must really love Seamus to be marrying him," Enya says with a somewhat dreamy look on her face.

"He's a wonderful man," I tell her honestly.

"It's crazy to think he'll be my brother-in-law in a couple of days," Enya says. "I'm sure he'll be the best husband."

I don't know how to respond to that. Enya happily munches away on another biscuit as a small part of me crumbles. We're so similar. Even the way we hide away our sadness is almost identical. She must've sensed my lack of conversation, so rather than sit in an uncomfortable silence, she begins telling me all about the process of making the honey shortbread.

"One of the most important things is that the butter is cold," she explains.

As she talks, my mind drifts to a day almost five years ago. I'd just turned thirteen when Seamus and I were called into my parents' office. Both of our parents were there. I can still hear the rain pounding on the window in the background and smell the fire burning in the fireplace. The chill from outside had permeated the walls of the manor, and while itchy and uncomfortable, the sweater I wore kept me warm. That moment is burned into my mind.

We were sitting on the couch, something we were never allowed to do. Mother and Brigit looked overjoyed. Father was silent, as usual. Fergus McNeillain refused to look at us. Thinking back, it must've been because of guilt. Seamus's father always was the only lord who actually had an ounce of empathy, even if he never acted on it. Mother told us we'd be getting married the day after I turned eighteen.

We thought it was a joke at first, but when Seamus asked, Brigit smacked his head and told him otherwise. I sat there in silence, realizing they were serious. Even at thirteen, I knew this wasn't right, but I could do nothing to tell them anything different.

They made it clear that this was going to happen whether we liked it or not. The last thing they had us do was to swear to keep the arrangement a secret. The Haddens learning about their plan could damage the deeply rooted power triangle of the isle. They had planned for us to act like we fell in love over time, plotting everything down to his proposal on my seventeenth birthday.

It wasn't until a little later that I learned the real reason why they wanted us to get married. In combining the families, they'd be able to use us to reestablish the monarchy that Queen Caitria had dissolved centuries earlier. In their minds, the monarchy would allow them to make all the decisions and to rule the isle as they saw fit.

Almost a year later, the morning after Father destroyed and burned my things, Shannon found me in the gardens with a face stained with tears. She put the pieces together pretty quickly after that. And while I've never told him, I'm positive Alan knows as well. Being as observant as he is, it'd be impossible for him to not have figured it out. Seamus and I can play our parts well in public, but neither of us is comfortable with any form of publicly displaying our supposed affection. The only person I wish knew about this farce of an engagement is Enya.

A knock on the door brings me back to reality and interrupts Enya's explanation of the different types of icing you can put on a shortbread.

Chapter 10

"Lord Seamus has arrived," Alan says as we open the door. "It's time to go to Lady Caitria's engagement celebration."

"Thank you, Alan," I tell him. He gives a nod before heading downstairs as we follow close behind.

"You look beautiful, by the way," Enya tells me with a wide smile. "Seamus won't be able to keep his eyes off you."

"Thank you, Enya," I say, grinning back at her. "You're looking lovely as well. Perhaps you'll catch the eye of a certain someone?" I suggest as I give her a look.

"Yeah, well, maybe," she mumbles as a light blush creeps into her cheeks. "We still don't know for sure if he'll even be there."

We make it to the bottom of the stairs, where Seamus is waiting for us. His cropped hair is smoothed back just enough to keep it out of his eyes. His dark pants are complemented by a dark green sweater. Judging by the exact shade of green, there's no doubt that Mother and Brigit picked out his clothes to match my dress.

"You both look wonderful," he tells us before coming over to me to give me the customary chaste kiss on the cheek. "Ready?" He offers each of us an arm.

We each take an arm and allow Seamus to escort us to the car that Alan pulled around to the front of the manor. After making sure Enya and I are safely inside, Seamus climbs in. Alan slowly drives away from the manor as we begin the short trip to the village. Enya looks out the window with wide eyes. I'm reminded that she rarely ever rides in the car, and I can't even remember the last time she was allowed to go into the village.

"How're you?" Seamus quietly asks so as not to draw Enya's attention.

"I've been all right," I reply with a small smile. "You?"

"I'm fine," he says. "Are you nervous?" he asks while looking at my hands, which are clenched tightly together.

"A little," I sigh, trying to relax. "There'll be a lot of people."

"I know," he replies, and I know he understands.

It'll be our first time in front of our people in such a casual way, and we are expected to act the part of a happily and very much in love engaged couple. The reality being such a stark contrast to what's expected is nerve-racking. While I hope this will be the last time we're seen by our people as a couple, we both need this to go well. At the very least, it'll help me keep everyone in the dark until after I'm far away from the isle.

"You look nice," I tell him, changing the topic to something much more mundane.

He smirks in my direction as we both know that our attire is intended to make a very obvious statement.

"Are you excited, Seamus?" Enya asks suddenly. It's clear that Enya is excited enough for all three of us, no matter how much she tries to hide it. "Cait's been in special etiquette lessons with your mum and Mother for the past few months."

"She has?" Seamus asks, flashing me a concerned look.

He knows from personal experience how harsh both of our mothers are by themselves and how toxic they are when they're together.

I give him a slight shake of my head as I don't want to talk about it. Mercifully, the wedding being two days away allows me to avoid those lessons.

"They never made me take any lessons. Dad said he'd rather spend time together, just us and your father, so that's what I've been doing," he tells her.

"That must be nice," Enya says.

I see her smile falter for a split second at the mention of Fergus actually wanting to spend quality time with his son. It's such a stark contrast to our parents, who only spend time with us whenever they have to. And even then, it's for the sake of making a good impression and showing people that we're this "happy family." Enya opens her mouth to say something else when we arrive at the outskirts of the village.

"Oh! We are almost there!" she exclaims as Alan slows the car to maneuver through the people.

The closer we get to the pub, the more people we see walking toward it. The usually narrow cobblestone streets are packed as people make their way toward the center of town. A number of them point at the car and wave as they step off to the side of the road to let us pass. Some of them even clap when they see us. I notice that the pub is overflowing as we slow to a stop in front of the entrance.

A stand-alone brick building, the pub is at the center of town. The numerous windows outside are beautifully decorated with flower boxes full of a variety of greenery. The two metal hooks jutting out each corner above the entrance are adorned with hanging flower pots. Several light-colored triangle banners decorate the double-sided doors. Above the windows are small lanterns illuminating a painted sign, *O'Shaughnessy's Pub.*

A tall man with cropped dirty blond hair in a loose-fitting knitted sweater walks out of the building and toward the car. Even though he looks to be in his midthirties, his joyful, childlike energy is palpable as he leans down to open the door with a wide smile.

"Fancy seeing you here, my young lord and ladies." He chuckles as he offers a hand to help us out, his breath forming a puff of air in the cold.

Enya slides out first, and I follow closely behind with Seamus exiting last. A chill runs through me as the icy breeze from the docks whips through the town. The man stands tall in front of us as Alan walks over with a smile.

"Long time, no see, old man!" The man chuckles when he sees Alan. They shake hands and greet each other before Alan turns to us.

"Lady Caitria, Lady Enya, Lord Seamus," Alan says, addressing each of us, "It's my great pleasure to introduce you to Cormac O'Shaughnessy. He'll be your host for the evening and has assured me that you'll be well taken care of."

"It's just grand to meet ya!" Cormac exclaims with a jovial laugh. "I'm glad to be welcoming ya to my humble pub."

"Thank you, Mr. O'Shaughnessy," I say with a smile as he takes my hand and holds it up to his face and bows slightly before releasing it. "We appreciate you welcoming us to your pub."

"Oh, think nothing of it," he says happily. His smile is almost infectious and feels so genuine. "And please, call me Cormac. Mr. O'Shaughnessy was my old fella."

"It's great to meet you, Cormac," Seamus says as he extends his hand toward Cormac, who takes the offered hand and gives it a hearty shake. "I've heard good things about you and your pub."

"Grand!" Cormac tells him. "I'd say it's bang on. Makes my job easier, what with bringing everyone together and all."

"It looks great," Enya says with a smile, and Cormac does the same bow while holding one of her hands. "Can we go inside?"

"Well, of course ya can!" he responds with a chuckle as he ushers us toward the door. "Come in, come in! I suppose ya young folks'll want to get inside and mingle? After all, I'd guess the whole Isle is here to celebrate with ya."

He opens the door for us and props it open as he waves us inside. Casting a quick glance up at the flowers, I see them perk up as I pass by. The closer we get, the louder the crowd gets. I can hear the sound of trad music playing inside over all of the voices and laughter. The fiddles and guitars are accompanied by a few long flutes called bombards, creating a welcoming and joyful atmosphere.

"Now, I expect ya to have a grand time," he tells us over the noise before we enter the crowd. "If ya need anything, just come find me at the bar, and I'll get ya sorted."

With the noise, each of us just gives him our own variations of smiles and nods. I feel Seamus slide a hand onto the middle of my back, and I push aside the nerves and awkwardness as we walk inside. We barely make it more than a few steps before we hear Cormac.

"Oye! I need everyone's attention!" he yells over the music, and the pub quiets down within a minute. "Let's give the warmest of welcomes to the couple of the hour, the young Lord Seamus McNeillain and Lady Caitria Callihan!"

A series of applause and whoops of cheer sound throughout the crowd as practically everyone in the room turns to look over at us. "As ya know, they're getting married in two days' time, so I expect ya to help them and young Lady Enya feel as welcome as possible."

"Of course!" a few people yell out.

"Grand!" Cormac chuckles. "Now, let's crack on,"

A few folks begin coming over to us. However, before they can say much of anything, Cormac leads us over to a round booth with a battered "Reserved" sign. He removes the sign as the three of us slide into the leather seats. "What'll ya be having?" he asks.

"I'll have the stout," Seamus says after a moment of thought.

"A wise choice! And for the ladies?" he asks as he looks at Enya and me.

"I will have whatever Seamus is having," I tell him, knowing the stout here, made near the McNeillain Manor, has a great reputation.

"Grand! And what'll ya have, Lady Enya?" Cormac asks.

"Can I get a half pint of elderberry cider?" she asks after a moment.

"Of course!" he says as he walks away.

"Good choice," I tell her, knowing the cider is made not too far from our manor.

As folks start coming up to us, Cormac brings us our drinks, and I take a sip of mine before I greet any more people. It's rich and smooth and is not overpowering with the hops. All in all, it really is a great stout.

Over the next hour, people from across Isle Draíocht come up to congratulate us, share their well-wishes, and let us know how excited they are for our lives together. As we talk with people, I'm happy to find that there's no decorum like Mother and Brigit drilled into me. Everyone's dressed so casually and comfortably that the three of us stick out with our nicer clothes. Mercifully, no one mentions it. During a brief lull in well-wishers, I notice Mab, the seamstress, standing off to the side of the bar.

"I'm going to get some water," I tell Seamus and Enya.

"Can you get me one too, please?" Enya asks as she looks through the crowd, undoubtedly searching for William.

"You got it," I tell her as I slide out of the booth.

Gerald Hadden walks over, giving me a nod before sliding into the booth to chat with Seamus. His shaggy hair falls into his brown eyes as he sits. The brief nod he gives Enya tosses it back into place as they begin to chat. Turning away from them, I walk over toward the bar.

I navigate through the crowded pub, accidentally bumping into a few people due to how packed it is. Someone bumps into me from behind, and I stumble when someone catches my arm. I look toward the person who helped me and find a tall, slender man with dark red hair.

"My apologies, Lady Caitria," he says, helping me catch my balance.

"No worries," I tell him with a smile.

He lets me go when I have my footing and goes back to his conversation as I continue toward the bar. I'm a few feet away when Mab notices me.

"Lady Caitria," Mab says as she greets me, looking a bit panicked. "I've been finishing up the final touches on your gown."

"I'm sure it'll look lovely," I tell her with a smile and see her slightly relax as I take a seat next to her.

"How long have you been a seamstress?" I ask Mab as Cormac walks over.

"Oh, for as long as I can remember," Mab responds in a cheerful voice. "My mum taught me how to sew as soon as I could walk. When I was old enough, mum and my nan let me help at the shop after school."

"It sounds like you all were really close," I say as a smile forms on my face.

"What can I get ya?" Cormac asks as he pours a pint for another patron, a curious look on his face.

"Two waters, please," I reply. He nods in response and goes off to grab them.

"We were," Mab says with a smile after Cormac walks off. "They've both passed now, but they taught me everything I know."

"I'm so sorry to hear that," I say softly. "They taught you really well. You make such beautiful clothes. We're lucky to have you."

"That's very kind of you. Thank you, Lady Caitria," she replies.

"I've always wondered how you get the fabrics from the mainland," I say as Cormac brings over two full pints of water before rushing off again to help the wave of people who've flocked to the bar. "Doesn't the ferry only come twice a week?"

"Oh, I usually go with Cormac to place those orders," she tells me before taking a swig of her cider. "Sometimes that ferry is so frustrating, and he needs to go to the mainland most mornings to get supplies anyway."

"Is that allowed?" I ask, surprised by this new piece of information. "I'd always thought people weren't able to leave the isle without the ferry."

"What?" she asks, and then her eyes go wide. "Oh, well, no. I suppose not? But the port master usually turns a blind eye to it. And

Cormac only ever lets us go with him, especially since he was able to restore one of the older ferries. It's a bit slower than the newer boats, but it's much easier for us to get the supplies we need. All we've got to do is show up, but that man wakes up so damn early that it's hard to keep up. You could set your watch to that man, though. He always leaves at the same time every morning. And it's not like he takes any tourists, not that we ever see many of those anyway."

I take a sip of water as she sputters over what she just said.

"I'm so sorry, my lady," she says quickly, her face turning red with embarrassment. "I didn't mean anything by it. It's just, well, you know."

"I get what you mean," I tell her with a small chuckle. "You're not wrong. Not many people visit from the mainland."

"Lady Caitria, may I ask you a question?" Mab asks after a moment.

"Of course," I say, feeling slightly nervous as to why she seems so hesitant.

Based on how she leans in enough so she can ask without being heard, the look of discomfort on her face, and the fact that she is wringing her hands together, I'm guessing it isn't something she asks lightly.

"Are you happy about the wedding?" she asks. "You seemed a bit upset at the fitting."

I feel tears prick my eyes at the question. No one's ever asked me that question. I stay quiet as I try to discreetly blink the tears away from my eyes. No matter what my answer is, it won't change anything. I'm so tempted to lie and say yes, but the look of genuine concern in her eyes as she watches me convinces me otherwise.

"What is happiness, really?" I ask quietly, not really having an answer. I can't even remember the last time I felt truly happy without the pressures from my parents looming over me.

"I see," she says quietly, looking away. "For what it's worth, I think you'll make a fine lady of Draíocht."

"Thank you, Mab," I tell her and give her a genuine smile.

She just returns the smile in response before downing the rest of her drink. "I've got to get back to the shop to finish your dress. I just have a few finishing touches left before it's ready."

She waves at Cormac before she turns to me one last time. "I'll bring it by tomorrow morning, yeah?"

I nod and wave as she walks away. I let out a small sigh before picking up the water glasses and walking back to the booth.

Chapter 11

I leave the bar, weaving through the groups of people, some patting me on the back and others giving their congratulations as I head back toward the booth. As I carefully place the waters down and take a seat next to Gerald, I notice our table has a new addition.

Sitting next to Enya is a young man with wavy black hair. It takes me a brief second to place him, but I soon realize this is the William she's been so excited about. They don't notice me right away, and I take the opportunity to watch Enya out of the corner of my eye. My heart warms as I see her smiling and laughing. It's so reassuring to see her so happy. What is even more reassuring, however, is the fact that William looks just as excited, if not more so, than she is. I try to glance over without her noticing, yet fail miserably.

"Oh, Cait," Enya says, meeting my eyes. "This is William Kelly."

"Hello, William," I say with a smile. "It's lovely to see you again."

"It's good to see you too, um, my lady," he responds, though his raised voice at the end tells me just how nervous he must be.

"Feel free to call me Caitria," I tell him, and I can see him relax ever so slightly.

"William's father is the carpenter who makes some of the furniture pieces in the manor," Enya says to break the awkward pause.

"He does a wonderful job," I reply, not entirely sure how to interact with him.

William looks between me and Enya as yet another slightly uncomfortable silence falls over us.

"So, William," Seamus says as he joins in on our conversation while Gerald looks on with curiosity. "What do you think of our Enya?" he asks, rather bluntly and to the point.

"And careful what you say," Gerald jokes. "She's like a little sister to us."

"She's one of the kindest people I've ever met," William says slowly. "And she's great to talk to." He clears his throat. "And I think she's the most beautiful person, inside and out."

"That's lovely," I reply softly enough that I am not sure whether anyone can hear me or not.

Enya turns scarlet at his words, and William gives her hand a squeeze. His face also turns a similar shade of red. Seamus gives me a pointed look, and I can tell we're both thinking the same thing. To hear how he talks about Enya is beautiful. She deserves that and all the happiness that comes with it. Gerald throws his arm around my shoulders and the other around Seamus's.

"Well, kids," he says, "I'd say this is a perfect time to dance, yeah?"

The three of us slide out of the booth, leaving Enya and William to talk. It's not much, but at least it's some privacy for them. We walk around the pub on our way toward the makeshift dance area at the opposite end. The tables scattered across the room are filled with patrons. Even the outside tables are full of people talking and laughing in the wintery chill. We give nods and waves in response to whoever instigates them, though almost no one comes up to us.

Cormac wasn't kidding when he said the entire Isle must be here. We even see Darina off to the side of the pub, though Seamus is cautious to keep clear of her on the off chance someone notices something and mentions it to our parents. Even from across the busy pub, I can see the love in his eyes whenever he sees her. When we reached the dancefloor, a number of people gathered around.

"Dance!" someone shouts from the crowd of people.

"Yeah! Let's have a dance!" another person shouts. Before we have a chance to decline or respond in any way, the crowd begins to chant.

"Dance! Dance!" they call, and the band behind us begins to play an upbeat song.

Seamus looks over at me, and I can see a smile form on his face as he gives me a playful bow. I laugh, pushing my nerves aside and taking his extended hand. We begin to move in time with the beat of the music, dancing around the space. The traditional Irish step dancing was taught to us from an early age, so we are easily able to move together to such a joyful tune. The crowd claps in time with the music, creating a fun layer of sound.

The pace picks up as the song goes on, and we continue to move in time with the music. I feel a smile form on my face as a laugh bubbles up inside me. We dance faster and faster in the small circular space. The more we dance, the more people join us. Soon, a large group is dancing alongside us. I lose track of time as we continue dancing, but eventually, the song ends. Several members of the crowd boo the musicians playfully, but we all leave the makeshift dance floor for the next group of people.

"I can't remember the last time dancing was so fun," Seamus says during the brief time it takes for the band to get ready for the next song. "Maybe we should talk with our mums about inviting them to the reception?"

"I think that's a great idea," I tell him.

A pang of guilt hits my heart as I say that. I'm silently hoping the reception will never happen, and I'll be far away from here by the time it's supposed to start. I'd love to be able to tell him that it's not going to happen, but he'd try and stop me. On the chance that I fail, though, trad music sounds like it would make a stressful day a little bit better.

As Seamus and I leave the dance floor, we're stopped every few steps by people. Most just want to give their congratulations, and a few want to ask us about our plans after we become a lord and lady of Isle Draíocht. I catch glimpses of Enya and William at the booth every now and then, their smiles warming my heart. When Seamus is in deep conversation with someone about something related to the future of stout production on McNeillain land, I take the opportunity to slip away and stand off to the side of the people congregated at the bar.

"What can I do ya for, Lady Caitria?" Cormac asks as he pours a few drinks from the tap nearby.

"I wanted to thank you for hosting us today," I say, and he gives me one of those infectious smiles.

"It's been a pleasure having you here," he tells me as he passes the drinks to a customer nearby.

"And I also wanted to thank you for helping out other people on the isle," I say, and he gives me a puzzled look in response. "I heard that you've been helping some shop owners get supplies."

"I see," he replies with a faint smile.

He nods toward the far corner of the bar, away from everyone, as he walks in that direction. I follow his lead, taking a seat on the stool as he pulls out a seat from the other side of the bar. Catching the eye of the other person working the bar, he gestures for them to take over while he sits.

"And how, exactly, did you come by this information, my lady?" he asks while picking up a few glasses to dry them as we talk.

"It's just something I heard here and there," I tell him, trying to be as vague as possible.

If he catches wind that Mab told me, he might stop helping her and other shops. With what I've seen over the past hour, he doesn't seem like the type of person to do that, but I know all too well how much people can hide under the surface.

"Do ya happen to know who else might've heard this?" he asks. I can see a flicker of nervousness in his eyes, but he hides it quickly.

While he doesn't ask directly, it's clear what he's asking. He wants to know if my parents or the other lords and ladies are aware of him helping ferry people to and from the mainland. The port master, keeper of meticulous records, ultimately works for them, so it could become a much larger issue should word get back to any one of them.

"I don't believe anyone was listening too closely," I reply.

"Ah," he mumbles. "Let me ask ya, do ya know if anyone would be interested in ya sharing such things?" he asks as he waits for my response.

It really is strange to see him so nervous around me. People have tiptoed around me before, but this is the first time I've ever seen someone look so nervous around me.

Can I really blame him? I think. *If word gets out, he'd be in a lot of trouble.*

"No, I don't think I'd see a need to share," I reply, and I can see him visibly relax.

"Grand," he says and then pauses, as if he wants to say something but is unsure how.

He looks closely at me, almost like he's analyzing every inch of my face. We sit in silence for a moment, and I notice his eyes move past me toward the direction of the booth we've been sitting at. He must've seen something because I can practically see something shift in the way he looks at me. It's a mix of curiosity and something else I can't quite place.

While he looks around, he grabs me a glass of water. "You know, I typically receive my kegs of the Callihan ciders early in the morning. Oftentimes, it comes in around a quarter to six."

"I am glad to hear it," I tell him, thankful he quickly caught on. "Have any mainlanders ever asked how they can get our cider outside of Isle Draíocht? It'd be nice to know if we could expand the business, and it'd help others on the isle to have the additional trade."

"That's a great question, my lady," he says as he gives me a pointed look. "I don't believe so, but I can ask anyone who comes in from the mainland." He pauses for a moment. "Have ya ever been?"

"Yes," I reply, knowing these next few minutes could make or break my escape plan. "Once, when I was quite little. I've always been interested in returning for a visit."

"Perhaps ya can go for a honeymoon?" he suggests. "Dublin is lovely in the spring."

"It'd be a nice visit. I've heard a few stories about people who go to the mainland and decide to stay. Something about finding new possibilities and opportunities and such," I reply.

"I know a few folks who've done that," he says slowly. "But a lot think it'd be dangerous to leave their home, or what all they'd be leaving behind. And it's not exactly easy to get back to the isle after ya leave."

"So I've heard," I say. "I'd imagine they've got a good reason, though."

Cormac glances over to one side of the room, and a thoughtful expression creeps over his face. I follow his gaze and see Seamus chatting with Darina and a few other people around our age. Seamus must've thought it'd be safe to go over to her, especially since Gerald was also there. While they're at opposite ends of the group, I can see the look in his eyes is one of pure admiration and adoration as he sneaks glances at her. I look away and focus on the water glass in my hands. One thing I have learned in this very short time is that Cormac, while kind, is very observant. It doesn't take long for him to look at me with sympathy in his eyes.

"It's admirable when people make sacrifices for those they love," he says in a soft voice I can barely hear.

I reply with a forced smile. "Perhaps that's why?"

"Maybe," he responds and goes silent in thought for a moment as he watches me.

After some time, a resolved look crosses his face. "I must apologize, Lady Caitria, but I'll be late to yer wedding. It'll be business as usual for me. Can't close the pub the whole day."

"Oh, that's all right," I reply with a genuine smile as I feel a sense of relief. A few moments later, Seamus walks over to me and places a hand on my shoulder.

"Thank you, Cormac," he tells him as he reaches a hand over the bar for a handshake. "Alan's just arrived to take us back to the manor."

"Aw, it would've been grand if ya could stay longer, but I understand," Cormac replies as he shakes Seamus's hand. He then looks at me and gives me a slight bow of his head. "Lady Caitria."

"Thank you, Cormac," I reply as I stand up off the stool. "It's been a pleasure."

We leave Cormac behind the bar as we walk over to Enya, who's still in conversation with William. They both seem very relaxed in each other's company. I hate to break up their conversation, but as she sees us walking over to them, her face falls, and she starts to get up. Clearly forcing a smile, she says goodbye to him, and I can see the disappointment on his face. All three of us walk out of the pub, waving goodbye to everyone as we make our way to the car Alan has pulled up near the entrance. He holds the door open as Enya and I slide in followed by Seamus. Once we are seated safely inside, he closes the door and heads to the driver's seat. Before starting the car, he turns around to look at us.

"Did you have an enjoyable time?" he asks as he shifts the car into gear.

"I did," Seamus says as he looks over to Enya and me.

"Absolutely," I reply absentmindedly.

"It was wonderful." Enya sighs as a blush creeps into her cheeks.

"Grand!" Alan replies as he pulls the car away from the curb and begins to make the drive back to Callihan Manor. "I'm glad to hear it."

We are all quiet during the quick drive. I know part of it is exhaustion, especially as it's been ages since we were last around that many people.

I find my mind spinning with this new information. I'd been struggling with how I'd actually leave the isle. With it being a ways away from the mainland, the only way across the deep water is on a boat, but the tourist ferry would be way too obvious, especially as they only ever leave in the middle of the day. Not to mention that the port master would never let me board one without clearing it with my parents. With Cormac's boat, I'd be able to leave virtually undetected. My parents wouldn't suspect a thing until it was too late.

"We're back," Alan announces as he slows the car to a stop in front of the manor. He opens the car door, and we all exit quickly, hurrying inside to get away from the cold. I walk toward the stairs when a voice stops me in my tracks.

Chapter 12

"Caitria," I hear Mother snap from the side of the staircase. "Where do you think you are going?"

"Apologies, Mother," I tell her as I walk over to where she stands with her arms crossed and a snarky look on her face. "It's late, and I assumed that the McNeillains had gone home."

"That was presumptuous of you," she responds with a bite in her tone. She looks over my shoulder at Seamus and gives him a wide smile. "Seamus, dear, will you and Caitria join us for a nightcap? Everyone's waiting."

"Of course, Lady Agatha," Seamus responds, and I see her face freeze.

"We'll be family soon," she says in an even voice, maintaining her painfully wide smile. "There's no need to be so formal."

"Yes, of course," Seamus responds as I see him roll his eyes after she turns around.

I stifle a smile as the three of us follow behind her. After all, the reason he still calls Mother "Lady Agatha" is because she yelled at him one evening a few years ago, saying how he needed to treat her with respect. She walks quickly to Father's office and opens the door. I take a breath to mentally prepare myself for what I am about to walk into before following Seamus inside. Enya follows quickly behind but is stopped in her tracks by Brigit McNeillain.

"Now, now," Brigit says in a condescending voice, the familiar scent of whiskey on her breath. "This is for adults only. Go run along to your room like a good girl."

I can see the hurt in her eyes, and I am about to say something when I feel Brigit place a hand on my shoulder, digging her thumbnail just behind my shoulder so no one notices. Icy fear shoots through me. It is a painful yet clear message that she expects me to remain silent. I know it'll only end badly for both Enya and me if I say something. Father and Fergus won't do anything, but Mother and Brigit will certainly retaliate. It wouldn't be the first time they've done it, but hopefully, this'll be one of the last times.

Hiding my fear, I try to silently apologize when Enya's eyes meet mine. She gives me a small smile, a glimmer of tears forming, as she turns around and quickly leaves the room. Brigit walks over to where Mother is sitting on the small couch by the fire while Father and Fergus are sitting off in the corner as they smoke their pipes.

"What was that child thinking?" Mother scoffs. "I specifically requested Caitria and Seamus, not her. She's so disrespectful, and she never listens."

"I know, Agatha," Brigit says, patting her hand with sympathy.

"Don't be too hard on her," Fergus says in a light tone. "Perhaps she just wanted to spend time with us? After all, we're going to be family the day after tomorrow."

"Perhaps, but Fergus, she's also just a child," Father tells him. "She should know by now that she's not welcome for a nightcap."

"Now," Mother says, looking directly at Seamus and me. "Have you and Seamus discussed your plans after you're married?"

"What plans are you referring to?" I ask hesitantly.

"Having children," Brigit says matter-of-factly.

"Raising an infant during the first few years of ruling is not for the faint of heart, Caitria." Mother chimes in. "It'll still be several years before your father and I step down and lord and lady, but you mustn't delay it or else it'll be too late."

"We haven't even had the wedding yet," Seamus says as my head spins. "I know we're expected to have children, but we still have time."

"The children will be your responsibility, Caitria," Father says sternly. "You'll be expected to have children to continue the family line. If it takes more than a few years, the people will lose faith in us and begin to think our family line will end with you, and that can't happen under any circumstances."

"Of course," I say numbly, absolutely mortified at the conversation.

"Having children will also help you connect with the people," Brigit tells us. "As a young family, you'll appear more relatable. You'll need that connection to gain their support."

"Wouldn't it be better to make those connections before children?" I ask in an even voice, trying to steer the conversation.

"She's right," Seamus chimes in. "If we build those bridges now, we'll have more support by the time we have children."

Father looks at me like I have grown a second head. Fergus, who's been silent on this entire conversation, gives me a look of sympathy. Mother and Brigit, on the other hand, share a look before they burst out laughing, almost maniacally. At that point, I notice just how much they've drunk. I've rarely seen them this intoxicated, but I can see it clearly now. Their laughter confirms it, and both of them have a few hairs out of place. In the stifling warmth of the room, their faces are flushed.

Alan arrives, interrupting their laughter and bringing Seamus and me each a cup of tea. We share a look before joining our parents. Seamus joins our fathers in the back of the room as they talk about business and politics. I, unfortunately, have to sit on the couch by the fire and listen to our mothers and their absurd ideas.

I gingerly perch on the edge of the chair near where they're sitting. Mother doesn't even bother to hide it when she pours whiskey in their tea. I take a sip from my cup as they begin talking about nothing of significance. Something about wedding details and vendors, the topic of future children all but forgotten. The change in topic brings some relief. If they're not involving me and I don't say anything, I'm safe. I tune them out like I usually do, focusing on the cup in my hands.

"What do you think of Enya and Gerald Hadden?" Mother asks Brigit.

I freeze in an instant. It's like a bucket of ice has been poured over me, and the panic sinks in. After everything they've put me through, they're seriously considering doing the same thing to Enya?

Why did I expect anything less? I think. After all, she's a year older than I was when they forced an engagement on me. A part of me crumbles at this, absolutely devastated by even the mention. However, another part of me is absolutely furious. The numbness sinks in as I continue listening to them.

"I think they'd make a fine couple," Mother continues after a sip of her whiskey tea. "We'd need Maureen and Angus Hadden to approve, of course, but they'd do well to get married."

"Oh, of course," Brigit says as she nods, drinking from her own glass. "He'd have to wait a few years, with her needing to grow up a bit, but we can just do what we did with Seamus and Caitria and start it early."

"Indeed," Mother replies, clearly pleased that her friend is in agreement. "It'd also be helpful in keeping the Haddens in line. What with our families being joined in marriage in a couple of days, I wouldn't put it past Angus Hadden to try and demand more power."

"Oh, absolutely!" Brigit agrees. Even listening to this makes my blood run cold and my stomach turn. "That snide little man has always been against our plan. A betrothal would certainly placate them."

"Not to mention we'd all be one family through our children and wouldn't need to wait for the next generation to start up the monarchy," Mother says with a grin.

I can't believe what I'm hearing. Are they really suggesting that they'd force their grandchildren to suffer through this if Enya and Gerald don't agree? They talk like it's the Dark Ages. Even the first Queen Caitria wasn't forced to marry anyone. Why should we be forced to marry each other? None of us want any of this.

As I try to remain calm, I can only hope that Angus and Maureen are smart enough to turn this ridiculous plan down. If they don't, I fully expect Gerald to put up a fight. However, I've got a sinking feeling that Mother and Brigit won't give them a choice in the matter.

"Oh, Agatha," Brigit cackles. "You're so diabolical. I love it!"

"Why thank you, my dear friend," Mother chuckles. "We'll need to train Enya to be a good wife and mother." She casts a brief sour look in my direction before looking back to Brigit. "I certainly hope she'll be more respectful than her sister, though."

"Yes," Brigit responds, refusing to even look over at me. "Hopefully, she'll be a much better pupil."

I stand up abruptly, without thinking. The air has left my lungs as I try to breathe. The heat of the room, all eyes suddenly on me, the silence that immediately falls, and the rising panic and rage that fight to be released are suffocating. I can't sit here another minute.

It's like a knife in my heart to know that they're planning to force Enya through the exact same thing they're doing to me. My sweet little sister, who's finally found a sliver of happiness, will be forced to give it away. They've never once shown her the care or love she deserves, and now they're going to take everything away. Both women both look over at me, and Mother sneers in my direction.

"Sit down, Caitria," she snaps as Father, Fergus, and Seamus look over at me as well. "You're being quite rude."

"No," I say simply, trying to keep my breathing under control. "I won't listen to this anymore."

"You will do as you're told," Mother says as her face begins to turn red. "You will sit down. I haven't given you permission to leave."

"I'm not asking for permission," I tell her, holding my head high as I take a step toward the door. Mother grabs my arm roughly, pulling me backward.

"You. Will. Sit. Down," she says slowly, and I can hear the threat in her voice.

"No," I tell her, placing my hand over my racing heart. The room is so quiet that you could hear a pin drop as everyone watches us. "I refuse to sit here and listen to your plotting."

"Sit down," Brigit demands as she stands. She grabs my tea from me and slams it down, the liquid sloshing about as she joins Mother. "I won't tolerate such disrespect and disobedience."

"You can't do this," I say as calmly as I can while Mother's grip tightens, her nails digging into my skin. "I won't let you do this."

I see her hand move out of the corner of my eyes and brace myself for the impact. A second later, I feel a hard slap across my face, accompanied by a loud crack. It takes the air out of me, and a metallic taste blooms in my mouth. Absolutely no one moves as the room goes completely silent.

"You will behave!" Mother bellows. The room is completely silent as everyone watches.

"No," I say again as I try to get my arm out of her grasp. "I refuse to turn a blind eye to this. You'll leave Enya alone."

However, another loud crack shoots across the room as Brigit slaps me. I hear the wooden creaking of a chair. Out of the corner of my eye, I see Father and Fergus looking away, almost ashamed by the sight. Seamus, on the other hand, looks completely shocked.

"You will obey us," she demands, and no one does anything. "Now sit."

"No," I say as I look at her defiantly. "I'm done."

I tear my arm from Mother's grasp. She slaps me with the back of her hand in response. I immediately feel the impact of the metal and jewels on her rings across my face. My cheek stings and burns from the shock. Her face blanches, and I know she must have left a mark on my face.

"I'm leaving. Now," I say definitely.

No one tries to stop me as I leave the room, slamming the door behind me. I've only gone a few steps when I hear voices being raised. I can't quite hear the words, but I recognize Father's voice reverberating through the heavy wooden door. In a second, I hear the door open and close before the sound of quick footsteps rushes toward me.

"Cait," I hear a voice say as I reach the stairs. I turn around to find Seamus right behind me. His eyes are wild and full of panic.

"What?" I ask, absolutely exhausted.

The last thing I want right now is to deal with another person, especially him. A tiny part of me had hoped he might step in and stop them from hitting me, but no such luck.

"Are you all right?" he asks, and I can tell he is looking for the right thing to say.

"Does it really matter?" I ask him as I feel a tear run down my cheek.

"It does," he tells me, and I can see him struggling to process what he just witnessed. "I knew they said mean things, but I never imagined they'd hurt you. Have they done this before?"

I look away from him, knowing that answering his question will make him feel worse. It started two years ago, but this is the first time they've done it with an audience. They wouldn't dare harm Seamus, but they never hesitated to hurt me. He never knew because I never told him. After all, it's not like I'd ever think he'd believe me. So, rather than say anything, I remain silent.

"Why didn't you tell me they hurt you?" he asks, and I can hear a sense of desperation in his voice. "I could've been there for you. I could've helped you."

"But you weren't," I snap, and then immediately feel terrible. "And what could you have done? Would you have stepped in and said something? Would you stop them or protect me?"

I see him open and close his mouth to answer, but we both know the truth. He wouldn't have been able to do anything for the exact same reason neither one of us has been able to end our engagement.

"If I'd known, maybe I could've protected…" he starts to say and then stops.

"Seamus." I sigh, not even wanting to hear the end of his thought. "We both know there's nothing you could've done. Don't put this on yourself," I tell him.

"Cait—" he says, and I cut him off by holding up my hand.

"I'm tired," I say softly. "Just, please, let it go." I begin to walk up the stairs.

Chapter 13

I feel absolutely exhausted by the time I get to the top of the stairs. As soon as I take that last step, I know this may be my best opportunity to run. I rush to my room to pack some essentials so I can leave. While the tears flow down my face, I begin to gather things. Digging through my closet, I find the small overnight bag that was supposed to be used for a honeymoon and set it aside, knowing that I won't be able to take anything other than what will fit in that bag.

I wipe away the tears from my eyes and focus in on my clothing. My face stings worse than ever, but I ignore the pain as I try to focus on the task at hand. Most of my clothing is relatively thin and not really good for the cold weather. I'm hoping I'll be able to get by with very little clothing, but I know I may be outside for a long period of time as I try to find a place to stay. I dig further back into the closet and come across a couple of thick sweaters.

I look down at the small bag and know I won't be able to bring more than one. I set the other aside and throw one in the bag while deciding that I should wear the other. Setting aside a few other shirts as well as an additional pair of pants, I sincerely hope I'll never be forced to wear a dress ever again. After throwing in a few more bits of clothing, I pack up the bag. It's not much, and I still have a small amount of room left. I lift it carefully to make sure it's not too heavy before setting it back down. Moving on to the bathroom, I grab a bar of soap, a toothbrush, and toothpaste, placing them at the top of the bag.

I move on to find paper and something to write with. The paper is easy to find, and I wrap up my few toiletries before packing them up, closing the bag securely around everything. It takes longer than I thought to find a writing utensil because the pencils and pens that I usually keep have somehow disappeared. I find nothing in the bathroom, but an idea comes to me that might resolve my issue. I rummage through a small cabinet in my closet and find an old fountain pen with a small ink vial. The ink has long since dried in its container, but after adding a little water and shaking it, it's just enough that I should be able to use it.

I sit down at the small table in my room and look out the window as I mentally prepare myself to write. I genuinely have no idea what to say, especially since I have no idea whether I'll ever come back or not. The first thing that comes to mind is Enya. I bite back tears as I begin writing. Knowing I don't have a lot of ink, I'm careful not to write too much. After thinking it over and over, I carefully began writing the letter, making sure to make no mistakes. It breaks my heart to know that this might be the last thing I give to her, but I know it'll be for the best.

Once written and drying, I move on to Seamus. I know this'll be hard for him to cope with, but I truly hope he'll finally be able to be with Darina. That being said, I know he'll need a lot of reassurance that none of this is his fault. I end it by thanking him for everything and wishing him years of happiness before setting that one aside to dry.

My final letter is to my parents. I know they'll probably never read it, and with the lack of ink, I'm not able to write a lot. Adding a small amount of water to thin it just enough, I stare at the final page, trying to think of what to write. Before the betrothal, they were good parents, so I decided that I'd write to the people they were, not who they'd become. It's difficult and more painful than I imagined, but it soon joins the others to dry.

I stand up and hide the letters in the back of my closet to finish drying along with my packed bag before heading into the hallway. Successfully avoiding the creaky spots on the floor, I make my way to Enya's room. No light shows below the door. The last thing I want to do is wake her up, but I know I'll always regret not saying good-bye. Taking a deep breath, I lift my hand to knock when the door creaks open.

"Cait?" she asks through the small crack in the door, opening it wider when she sees me on the other side.

Her eyes are red, and I know she has been crying. Enya looks at me for less than a second before her eyes go wide. She grabs my wrist and gently pulls me inside her room. After guiding me to one of the chairs in her room, she quickly grabs a cloth and wets it with water before sitting in front of me.

"What happened?" she asks as she gently dabs my cheek with the cloth.

I flinch as it stings but say nothing, feeling ashamed. I'm ashamed that, even though I did nothing to help her earlier when they treated her so harshly, she's taking care of me.

"It's nothing," I tell her without thinking and then look away. Enya purses her lips, and she suddenly looks older than her fourteen years.

"It's not nothing. Please don't shut me out," she pleads, and I can hear the hurt in her voice.

She starts crying again as she helps clean my face. I find it so hard to form the words, but she deserves to know.

"Mother," I choke out as I feel tears start streaming down my own face. "Brigit, too."

"In front of Father and Fergus? Was Seamus there?" she asks, and I see her face go pale. "Why didn't anyone step in?"

"They just sat there," I whisper, and she takes a shaky breath as she sits down next to me.

"How can they still allow this to happen?" she mumbles in shock before turning to me. "They've never made you bleed before. It's getting worse."

"No wonder Mother looked like she was going to be sick," I say with a harsh laugh, and I feel like I can breathe a little.

With it only being two days before the wedding, she must be frantic, trying to figure out what to tell people about the mark that wasn't there earlier. I get some satisfaction in that as I grab Enya's hand and squeeze it.

"I need you to promise me that you'll fight," I tell her. "You've got to stand up for yourself. I won't be able to live with myself if they do the same thing to you."

"What?" she asks, and she crouches in front of me. "What're you talking about?"

"I need you to promise me, Enya," I say as I look her in the eyes. I can see her fear and anger for what they did to me, but also a clarity.

"You aren't making any sense, Cait," Enya says, even though I can see her starting to put the pieces together. "What did they make you do?"

"I'm so sorry," I tell her as I can see the realization dawn on her. "I wanted to tell you sooner."

She's quiet for a moment, holding the bloody rag in one hand and my hand with the other.

"You never wanted to marry Seamus. Did you?" Enya asks quietly with an unsteady breath. I shake my head in response and look down at my hands.

"Why didn't you tell me?" she asks, and I can hear a crack in her voice. I don't even need to look to know she is crying.

"Because they made me swear not to," I say simply, knowing it's a hollow excuse. "And I knew you'd try to do something about it. But if they were focused on me, they'd leave you alone."

"Why do I need to fight?" she asks, her voice trembling, and I can see the fear and heartbreak in her eyes. "What are they going to do?"

"They're going to try and force you into an arranged marriage," I tell her, trying my best to keep my voice steady as tears begin to fall from my eyes.

However, the moment I see her face fall, I can't hold back anymore. I let the tears flow freely, and we cried together. My cheek stings, but I don't care. She throws her arms around me, continuing to cry. I hold her as she shakes from her tears. There's nothing but pure heartbreak and pain, something I know well.

I have to leave, I think. *It's the only way to make them see. They'll all see then, and they'll never do this again.*

Seeing her so upset makes my decision even more important. I wish I could take her away with me, but I know it wouldn't be safe. As much as it hurts, I know that she'll be safest here. If nothing changes, they'll continue forcing things on us.

Enya continues crying as I help her to bed. Tucking her in and giving her a kiss on the forehead, I sit by her side until she begins to calm down. I brush her hair away from her eyes, wiping away a few stray tears along the way.

"Who?" I hear her mumble. The look on her face is one I recognize all too well—the same numbness I see on my face most days.

"Gerald Hadden," I tell her, trying to be calm.

"I guess it could be worse," she replies softly, and I hate it. "At least he's nice."

Enya drifts off to sleep soon after that. Hearing the sad acceptance in her voice before she fell asleep shatters my heart. I watch her for a moment longer, taking in what might be the last time I see my sister. Tear stains on her pillow continue forming as she cries in her sleep. I can do nothing to help her now. The only thing I can do is hope that they'll realize they can't control us.

As soon as I'm sure she won't wake up, I sneak out of her room and back to mine. I pull a warm sweater over my head before grabbing the bag. I sling it over my shoulder before placing the letters on my desk. After slipping on my shoes, I listen in the hallway for any indication that anyone's awake.

I'm greeted with complete silence. For the first time, I feel like I actually have the possibility of being successful. I sneak down to the kitchen, grabbing a flashlight, before carefully making sure the door closes silently behind me. I quickly make my way toward the edge of the forest, knowing I'll have help as soon as I get past the first few trees. The path is much more difficult, however, as it's darker than normal tonight.

Once I reach the top of the hill, an ominous feeling washes over me. Something feels off. The forest looks darker than usual, with a thick layer of clouds rolling through the moonless sky, and I can hear some of the branches of the trees creaking. The longer I look at it, the more it feels like something is in the trees, something dangerous. It almost feels as if something is watching me.

As I walk past the first few trees, a wave of dizziness hits me, and I stumble. Falling to the ground, my hands scrape on the rocks and roots. A shriek pierces the air as the nausea takes over. A cold sweat quickly soaks my sweater, and my skin feels clammy. Something is seriously wrong, but this may be my only chance to escape. I'm not going to let it go to waste and try to take another step when a crack of lightning lights up the sky.

My blood runs cold as fog rolls across the ground. In the distance, it begins to take the shape of a woman. I'm frozen in fear at the sight of her. I've heard about them in stories. Women of the fog whose shrieks are an omen of death and pain. The unnatural glow around her only emphasizes her eyes, or rather, the black holes where her eyes should be. Her dark hair floats around her head like she's underwater, only making her more terrifying to see.

Cocking her head to the side, she gives me a smile that takes up the bottom half of her face, putting her sharp teeth on display. The banshee begins to drift toward me with a hand stretched out.

"Come to me, little one," she says with a voice that sounds like glass breaking. "The witch wants to see you."

I'm completely frozen in fear at the sight of her. I know I need to run far away, but I'm stuck in place, unable to move no matter how much I will it. She's close enough now that I can feel the chill emanating from her. Before she can reach me, I feel something grab my arms and quickly pull me away. With what little strength I have, I look up to see two large birds. They drag me to the tree line, throwing me a few feet out of the forest. They perch next to each other on a thick branch overhead, looking down at me with their familiar golden eyes.

"You must leave the forest," Glac tells me, breathless.

"It isn't safe for you here," Sorcha says with an urgent tone. "Run as fast as you can, and whatever you do, do not look back."

Wobbly and unbalanced, I try to get my feet under me. I grab hold of the strap of my bag, still secured over my shoulder, before stumbling down the hill back to the manor. I hear a shriek behind me and know the banshee might not be alone. Moving as fast as my feet will carry me, I trip over my own limbs as soon as I cross into the garden. My head begins to pound as I try to stand. Then the rain starts. I somehow manage to stand up and throw myself into the kitchen. However, once inside, I'm frozen as a wave of pain flows over me.

"Lady Caitria," I hear a voice say in a frantic whisper.

My eyes crack open, and I find Shannon standing over me. When she sees me, her eyes go wide, and she mumbles something before running away. Yet another flood of dizziness and nausea assault my senses, accompanied by a splitting pain shooting through my head. I can hardly keep my eyes open, but I can hear the sound of multiple footsteps approaching me.

"It'll be all right, my lady," I hear Alan say from somewhere close by.

Not even a second later, I feel two people grabbing my arms as they help me stand. They help me up the stairs without a moment's hesitation. I try to keep my feet under me but can hardly get enough air in my lungs, let alone support my own weight. All the while, we have an unspoken agreement to be as quiet as possible. It feels like hours before we finally arrive at our destination.

Once there, a light blinds me as they help me sit on the floor. Cracking my eyes open, I'm relieved to see that it's my bathroom. I hear Shannon give Alan some instructions as the nausea becomes too much.

"Bring me a cup of hot water and one of the packets from the small wooden box under the sink," she tells him, tying my hair out of the way. "We'll need an extra towel and some salt as well."

"Right away," he says as he rushes out the door.

I feel Shannon remove my bag from my shoulder, taking it out of the bathroom before coming back with a blanket. She folds it and places it under my head as I begin to shake. I try to keep my mind clear as I feel the world fade in and out.

The next thing I know, I'm being sat up as Shannon helps me drink a bright red liquid. It's bitter, and I'm about to spit it out when she holds my mouth closed.

"You must drink, Caitria," she urgently says as Alan dabs the sweat from my face.

The world fades away again, and when I open my eyes once more, they're cleaning my hands and face. Shannon, noticing my eyes open, grabs the bitter drink again and gets me to drink a little more.

The next time I open my eyes, I notice they're both standing nearby.

"Go back to bed, Alan," Shannon says. "She's gone through the worst of it. I'll keep watch just in case and will call you if she needs anything."

"Very well," he says before walking away.

All too soon, the world fades away once again as I'm thrown into darkness.

Chapter 14

When I open my eyes again, I'm back in the forest. However, it's not like the forest I know. In front of me is a single large, ancient tree, illuminated by a dim white light seemingly from nowhere. The branches move softly in a nonexistent breeze. A dark fog covers the roots and the ground, and I smell something burnt in the air. Something feels dangerous about this place. I look down and notice that I'm wearing a long black dress. Its fine details remind me of spiderwebs.

A young man steps out from behind the tree. He's handsome, with an air of danger around him. He reaches his hand toward me, and that's when I notice the dozens of small scars covering his hands. I try to take a step back, trying to create some distance, but I am unable to move. That only makes him laugh, a cruel, harsh sound.

"You can't run, little human," he tells me in a smooth, deep voice. "You wouldn't like me chasing you."

He takes a step closer and grabs my chin. I try to get out of his grasp but feel another set of hands tightly gripping my arms. I look at their owner to find another young man, almost identical to the first. His touch feels cold, and I notice his fingertips look almost black.

"You mustn't tease her, Dain," the man says, his voice like a whisper. "Mother said not to harm her."

"What Mother doesn't know won't hurt her," another voice chimes in, this one sounding sharp.

I look up and see yet another man sitting among the branches of the old tree. Looking the same as the other two, he gives me a smile that makes my skin crawl. It's too wide to be normal, and his teeth are jagged and abnormally large. He jumps down off the tree and joins the others.

The three men surround me, and I feel as though I might suffocate as they all slowly inch closer. No matter how hard I try, my legs are frozen. A cold sweat covers my skin as terror races through me. I try to open my mouth to say something, but no words come out. With every passing second, it gets harder and harder to breathe. Their cruel smiles only serve to increase my terror. I feel utterly helpless.

"Dain, Dub, Dother," a woman's voice snaps. "Please give our guest some space."

"Yes, Mother," all three men say in unison, each moving at lightning speed to stand behind a woman who appears from a black fog.

"Now, let me look at you," she says as she drifts closer. The air around her is cold and still. Her fingers are long and slender, grabbing my chin lightly. "You look just like her."

I open my mouth to try and speak, but again, no sound escapes. She lets out a cruel laugh at the sight of me as she takes a step back.

"What can possibly be the matter?" she asks, taunting me. "Will you not speak?"

Something in the way she talks irks me. For just a moment, I feel incredibly angry, and that overrides my fear. Not wanting to give her the satisfaction of watching me fail to say anything, I decide to keep my mouth shut. Raising my head to meet her bright red, cat-like eyes, I realize something. This woman looks eerily familiar.

I can't quite place it but don't have time to dwell on it. She lets out an exasperated huff as she reaches for my face. The fear that was held at bay now returns with a vengeance as her blackened fingers, adorned with claws, fly at me. I try to duck, but I can't move a muscle. However, she grabs at something on my face, barely grazing my skin. As she pulls her hand away, I notice she's holding a puff of black smoke.

"Speak," she demands.

"Who are you?" I ask, trying to make sense of this situation. "Why am I here?"

"You are here," she says, taking a step away from me as she circles me. I try to move but only manage to shift slightly in place, my arms and legs frozen. "Because I brought you here."

"You see, I'd like to make you an offer," she whispers against my ear in a sickly sweet voice, her breath smelling like death as it tickles my neck. "I need your little gift, and in return, I'll give you the power to make sure you're never powerless again."

"What are you talking about?" I ask, trying to stall as I attempt to figure out who she is.

"You have a gift, Caitria," she says, her voice dripping in venom as she once again stands in front of me. "And I need it. Your Sight. And the charm from my dear sister."

It's like something clicks at that comment, and I realize why she seems so familiar. This woman, filled with malice and fury, looks identical to the Cailleach. So if that's her sister, this is someone more dangerous than I imagined.

"You're Carman, aren't you?" I ask as an icy chill runs down my spine.

"Very good, little human." She sneers at me.

Fear courses through my veins at this omission. Carman is in very few stories, but when she is, they're full of death and destruction. The scorned sister of the Cailleach, she's a very dangerous and powerful witch. With her sons, she almost destroyed the world centuries ago with the intent to plunge it into darkness. However, in the stories, she and her children were locked away in a place they could never escape.

"How is this possible? How are you here?" I ask as I take a step away from her, amazed for a brief moment that whatever kept me in place is now gone.

"Wouldn't you like to know?" she teases as she takes a step closer to me. "But it matters not. All you need to know is that I can help you. Now, do we have a deal?"

She smiles at me, extending a hand toward me. Her eyes are filled with hatred, and her smile makes my skin crawl. As she takes another step closer, the smell of rancid smoke fills my nose, and it takes everything in me to not let it show. I look at her warily as she waves her hand over my eyes. My mind goes blank, and images begin to flash through my mind.

The first thing I see is my parents bowing to me as I sit on a throne of stone. A crown sits on my head as the entire Isle bows to me. Smoke clouds the land in the distance as the forest burns in the background. A cruel smile adorns my face as Carman stands to my side, her sons on the other.

The next image is of my hands emanating a darkness, stopping Mother from hitting me. I watch as I strike her, knocking her down. Roots spring up from the ground and pull her under until just her face remains. Her screams echo in my ears as I watch her get pulled beneath the dirt. The glowing red in my eyes is almost identical to Carman's.

The final image is of a number of men trying to woo me. Carman's sons stand behind me as every single man is dismissed. In the corner, Seamus sits in a cage, beaten and bloodied. The same darkness, glowing eyes, and cruel look on my face remain as flowers decay on the floor.

I gasp as I'm brought out of it and back to the dark woods. Carman is nowhere to be seen as her sons watch me from near the tree across from me.

"Well?" I hear her ask from right next to my ear. In the blink of an eye, she moves around to stand in front of me, her sons behind her once more. "What do you say?"

"No," I whisper as the images have been burned into my mind. No matter how much I try, I can't get them out of my thoughts. "That'll never be me."

"What?" Carman snaps. "It's everything you've dreamed of."

"It's not," I say, a bit louder than intended. "I never wanted to be cruel. I don't want power. "

"I see," she says as a stoic look takes over her face. "So it's a no, then?"

"I'll never help you," I whisper as my head begins to pound.

Sweat drips down my forehead, and I can hear her cackling. I think back to what the Cailleach said and try to see if I can somehow connect with the tree behind the four of them. I strain as I try to make some part of it move. I hear cackling as I continue trying to focus.

"Mother, look," I hear a smooth voice say with a cruel amusement. "She's trying to use her powers. How quaint."

"She's weak," a whispery voice says with a harsh laugh. "Try as you might, little human, but you're weak."

I don't respond to their taunts. Instead, I close my eyes, shifting my focus. My head begins to pound, and sweat beads on my forehead as I hear her cackling. The first thing that pops in my head is what's waiting at home. Enya and her smiling face were so full of love and optimism. I can hear Seamus laughing at a story long since passed. Shannon, with her motherly nature and unyielding kindness, even when some people never appreciate it. And Alan, who is the closest thing I have to a father, showing me a quiet love and kindness my entire life.

I think about how much I need to leave the isle. Seamus and Darina can only be together if I leave. They deserve a life filled with love and happiness. Enya and her newly forming romance with William might be doomed from the start unless I leave. Mother and Father, for all their faults, might be able to try again at being the parents Enya deserves if I force them to see what they've done. Even Gerald, who's always been there for me even though we've hardly seen each other these past few years, could avoid an arranged marriage and have a chance at finding someone who will love him for who he is.

Suddenly, the cackling grows silent and begins to fade. I hear the creaking of wood but don't open my eyes as I hear snarling. An angry shriek pierces the air, followed by a flash of light. Then, the world goes quiet. When I finally open my eyes again, I'm relieved to see Shannon squatting next to me.

"Oh, thank goodness," she says as she sighs in relief. "I thought you had left us for a minute."

My throat feels like sandpaper as she brings the red liquid to my lips, and I take a sip. She dabs the sweat from my forehead, and after a minute, I'm able to sit up on my own. The nausea and dizziness have all but vanished as I take a few deep breaths. Shannon watches me in silence, a protective hand placed on her belly. Soon, I feel ready to stand, and she helps me up.

"I put your bag in your closet and hid the letters under your pillow," she tells me softly once I'm upright.

"Thank you," I tell her, unable to meet her eyes.

She helps me over to the bed, and we both take a seat on the edge, unable to say anything. After a few minutes, she opens her mouth to say something. I quietly wait as she closes it again.

"You'll need these," she says softly after a moment. Reaching into the pocket of her dress, she holds out a number of tea bags toward me. "It's a family recipe. My mum made it to help those who were attacked by dark spirits."

"How…" I start to say. However, I don't finish that question. Shannon's mum was known as a medicine woman. Some thought her crazy to still believe in the old ways, but in this instant, I'm extremely grateful she taught her daughter her ways.

"Thank you," I say after a minute.

She pats my hand in response before she stands up.

"I'm naming her Shauna," Shannon tells me, rubbing her belly. "Send me a letter when you get to where you're going, yeah?"

"Of course," I agree as tears prick my eyes. I stand up on shaky legs and give her a hug. "I'll miss you."

"I'll miss you too," she says, giving me a little squeeze before letting go. "We won't say anything."

"Thank you," I tell her as she walks out the bedroom door.

As soon as she's gone, I somehow manage to slip out of my dirty, damaged clothes and into pajamas. Resolving to leave tomorrow after everyone goes to sleep, I curl up under the blankets of my bed and drift off to a dark, dreamless sleep.

Chapter 15

I wake up the next morning, my muscles more sore than they've ever been. My head pounds, and my throat is dry. I hear a familiar clicking sound as I open my eyes. The bright light streaming through my window hurts as I sit up in bed. A disgusted scoff causes me to whip my head toward the side of my bed.

Awaiting me is the unpleasant sight of Mother standing over me with her arms crossed over her chest, tapping her foot against the floor. She looks angry, and I immediately panic. Did she see something that would ruin my escape plan? A cold sweat covers my skin as a wave of nausea and fear rolls over me.

"Where have you been?" she demands, not moving an inch as I climb out of bed.

"Does it matter?" I ask her with a sigh, my voice sounding scratchy.

"What is wrong with you?" Mother seethes as I grab a glass of water from my bathroom sink. "You embarrassed our family in front of the McNeillains last night. You have the audacity to disobey both Brigit and me, and now I've got to figure out how to fix your face for the wedding tomorrow. How dare you act so disrespectful?"

"How dare I?" I ask in a calm voice, feeling something snap inside of me. "Don't forget that you're the one who gave me these."

"Oh, save your dramatics, Caitria," she sneers. "It doesn't suit you."

"I'm being dramatic?" I force a laugh. "Do you hear yourself right now? You're forcing Seamus and me to get married. We never had a choice. We've been forced to give up our lives for your stupid power play, and I'm the dramatic one? What have we ever done to deserve this?"

"You know very well what you did to deserve that," she says in a menacing voice as she grabs my chin forcefully. She turns my head so she can see the marks on my cheek before letting me go. "Those blemishes are rather unfortunate. But no matter. We'll tell the makeup artist to cover it."

"Is that all you can think about?" I ask, feeling like I must be the only sane one in the room. Angry tears prick my eyes as her cruelty surprises me yet again. "I was bleeding because of you, and all you can think about is covering it up. Do you even care?"

"Quiet," she demands in a sharp voice. Before I can even process the sight of her hand moving, she backhands me, hitting the same cheek as last night. I flinch but don't move any more than that. I refuse to give her the satisfaction.

"I refuse to hear any more of your nonsense. I will not be questioned." She sneers again before she walks to my bedroom door. "You will get married tomorrow, and you will smile and be happy. Do you understand me?"

"How can you be so heartless?" I ask, no longer caring what she does to me. "Is this what you'll do to Enya? Force her to obey you and punish her when she doesn't?"

"If I must," she snaps. Her face continues growing redder at the mention of my sister. A vein bulges in her neck, and her fury permeates the air.

"No," I say as I feel something overcome me as I reach up and touch the pendant hiding under my shirt. "I refuse to let you harm her."

"You really think you can tell me what to do?" She laughs harshly, striding back over to me. "Tell me, Caitria, what will you do to stop me? You have no power."

"I won't let you do this," I tell her, tears of anger rolling down my face. "Enya deserves to live her life the way she wants." I feel a strange force flowing through me as my fingers tingle.

Rather than say anything, however, Mother's eyes go hazy for a split second. Her face relaxes, and I can barely hear her mumble something so softly under her breath. She's back to her senses almost immediately, shaking her head for a brief moment.

"You will not leave this room. Maybe then, you'll learn your lesson." She holds a key that I recognize as the one for my door. "I expect you to be ready to respect and obey me first thing tomorrow." She slams my door shut at that, locking the door, and I know she has taken the key with her.

I feel my breathing speed up as I begin to panic. I have no way out of here. She's struck me more times than I can count, but this is a new low. Tears begin to spill down my cheeks. I know I don't have time to dwell on my emotions right now. If my plan is going to succeed, I have a lot of work to do.

Taking a deep breath, I do my best to calm down before assessing the situation. Finding the clothes from last night, I give them a once-over. The pants are torn at the knees, and the sweater is caked in mud. It's a lost cause to try and repair them. I shove them under my bed and decide to shower before figuring out what to do.

After a quick shower, I inspect my hands. Thankfully, the scrapes aren't that severe. Shannon and Alan did a good job cleaning and caring for my wounds. I look down and see bruises forming on my knees, but mercifully, there's no broken skin. I lightly touch one and flinch at the tenderness.

At least it's not worse, I think.

Finally, I force myself to look in the mirror. My makeup from the night before wasn't ever fully removed, as is evident by the dark smears beneath my eyes. I clean my face with a damp cloth, removing the collage of smudges, and cringe at the sharp pain as water touches my cheek. I take a deep breath as the scratches send a hot, pulsing pain when I gently wipe off the dirt. I clench my teeth together and try to ignore the sensation while I finish cleaning my face.

I put the cloth down and leaned toward the small mirror to inspect the few dark scratches. They're swollen up a bit more than I thought. I gently touch the inflamed skin and wince as pain radiates from the contact. It doesn't look infected, but the marks are definitely not minor scratches like Mother insinuated. It's certainly not something that the basic makeup I have would come close to covering. It's not bleeding, though, which is more than I could've hoped for.

I feel numb as I continue looking at the marks. It may have been a surprise to Mother to see the consequences of her actions, but I've grown all too familiar with her handiwork. She's left marks everywhere in the form of bruises and scrapes to the mental scars that span years. A part of me feels enraged that someone could do such a thing to their own child. However, Mother started seeing me as a pawn for her own gain years ago.

I take a deep breath before working up the energy to figure out what to wear later tonight. The light chill in the manor is nothing compared to the frigid cold that whips across the isle after sundown. Before I can take more than a few steps toward the closet, I hear a knock at the door. I quickly throw on a robe as the muffled jingling of keys sounds on the other side of the door. The lock clicks right before the doorknob creaks as it turns.

What more could she possibly want? I think, feeling exhausted by even the thought of seeing Mother again.

Every muscle in my body tenses up as the door slowly scrapes open. I hold my breath, waiting for Mother to barge in. Maybe this time, she's brought Brigit to back her up. The seconds pass by in what feels like a small eternity. However, a large black bag inches into the room, followed by a cheery voice.

"Hello, Lady Caitria," Mab excitedly says as she shuffles in. "Are you ready for your final fitting?"

"Of course," I say with a sigh of relief.

The door slams closed almost as soon as she hangs the dress on my bathroom door. A click from the door gives a clear message that we are locked in. Mab makes sure the dress is secured before turning toward me. Her eyes get wide at the sound before she turns to look at me with concern that only grows once she sees my face.

"What happened here?" she whispers as she rushes over to me. Reaching out to touch the scratches on my face, she stops before she makes contact. Tears quickly form in her eyes as she brings her hand to her mouth.

"I'm fine," I tell her as I place a hand gently on her arm.

"That's not fine. How can you say this is fine? Nothing about that is okay," She insists in a fast whisper, anger filling her voice. "How could they treat someone like this? This is an outrage."

Seeing her emotion, I almost crack and let my own make an appearance. Her anger on my behalf is palpable. While I hate the feeling of being seen as pitiful, I'm overwhelmed at knowing someone sees my situation for what it is. We both know that while just the two of us are in this room, we're anything but alone. She clears her throat and puts on a smile that is very clearly forced.

"Let's make sure your dress fits, yeah?" she asks, her voice wavering slightly.

I nod in response, unable to talk as I swallow away the lump that's formed in my throat. She lays out the dress, helping me find my footing. My stomach lets out a growl in protest as she pulls up the gown. Mab's hands pause in response, and while I don't look at her, I know she's trying to maintain her composure. She makes a discreet attempt to wipe away a tear without me noticing, but I see it. Neither of us says anything as she makes sure every inch of the dress fits me properly.

Once she has given me and the dress a thorough examination, she gives a small nod before helping me out of it. She is usually talkative to some extent, so her complete silence is unnerving for me. I quickly slip back into my robe while she carefully places the dress back in the garment bag, hanging it on the outside of my closet door. She then comes over and pulls me in for a tight hug.

"You deserve so much better," she tells me softly before letting me go. I see fresh tears on her cheeks, and she doesn't hide it when she brushes them away.

"A cold cloth on your face will help, and you'll need to be careful with your makeup tomorrow to make sure you don't get anything in those cuts." She pauses to clear her throat as she places a hand on my shoulder, giving it a light squeeze. "You won't be able to cover those, so Lady Agatha'll need to accept that they will be visible."

"Thank you, Mab," I tell her with a nod. "For everything." I feel myself getting choked up as a sharp and distinct knock sounds at the door.

"I wish I could do more," she tells me as she walks to the door that Mother has just unlocked.

As soon as Mab steps out of my room, Mother is quick to lock the door once again. I notice that, before the door closes, she completely refuses to look in at me. While it hurts, I take a mental image of her, knowing this will very likely be the last time I see her. With the metal click indicating that the door lock is secured, I slump down on the floor.

My stomach aches with the lack of food, but I ignore it, knowing there's no way Mother will let me have anything. The next time I'll be able to get any food will be the moment I sneak out. I glance out the window and sigh as the sun is relatively high in the sky. I still have some time before I'll be able to safely sneak out of the manor.

At least I have time to figure out how to get out, I think, trying to focus on the positives. I set my sights on the door, knowing the only way out is through that locked door.

The small window in the bathroom is high enough that I can't climb through it. The window in my bedroom doesn't open far enough for me to climb through. Not only that but being up on the top floor prevents me from being able to get to the ground safely even if I was able to climb through either of the two windows. I know Mother won't unlock it herself. She locked me in here to "teach me a lesson," and I know that no amount of convincing will get her to open the door. The only way out is to figure out how to unlock the door from the inside.

After throwing on a clean pair of pants and a shirt, I crawl over to the door and look through the keyhole. It's large enough that I can fit something in there to unlock it. Looking over toward my open closet, I stand up and walk over to grab a hat pin from a small cup on the vanity. I look from the pin to the door and decide I need to test it on the bathroom door. After all, the locks all use a similarly large iron key. I can only hope the lock would be similarly picked open.

Carefully holding the metal pin, I gently maneuver it into the lock. Keeping my ear against the door next to the lock, I listen for any sounds. A small clicking sound tells me I'm going in the right direction. I wiggle it around a little to see if that will do anything to lock the door, but no such luck. I grab another hat pin and a broach with a long pin before trying again.

It takes a while, but I eventually find the right combination of objects and movements I need to lock the bathroom door. I practice unlocking it and locking it, getting quicker and quicker at setting the pins into place. Each and every time, it gets easier and easier to do until, eventually, I decide to carefully try it on my bedroom door. To my great surprise, the bedroom door unlocks quite quickly, and I crack it open carefully to make sure I was, in fact, successful. I let out a sigh of relief at my success before locking it back to prevent any potential suspicion in the unlikely event that anyone should try to open the door.

With that final obstacle figured out, I decide to lie down and get as much sleep as I can. I set my alarm for three in the morning and crawl under the blankets. I close my eyes and try to sleep. After a while of tossing and turning, I fall into a deep sleep.

Chapter 16

A beeping sound wakes me up and I shoot out of bed, feeling groggy and slightly lost as I realize it's now or never. I slip into the sweater I had set aside yesterday before crawling into bed and get out the three letters I had written from their hiding place. Quickly and quietly, I slip my bag onto my shoulder and grab the small amount of money I have as well as the few pieces of jewelry I decide to sell on the mainland.

This time, I'll succeed, I think. *With the wedding later today, it's my last chance.*

I touch the pendant from the Cailleach that hides under my sweater and silently plead with the universe that this plan will work. I take one last look around my bedroom, soaking in the feeling of familiarity before I unlock the door using the various pins. It only takes a few seconds before I hear the tell-tale click.

I place the letter for Mother and Father neatly on my made bed before I open the door carefully to ensure I don't make a sound. After grabbing my shoes and locking the door behind me, I sneak to Enya's room down the hall. I slip her letter under the door before I head down the stairs, making sure to be as quiet as I possibly can. As soon as I reach the kitchen, I slip on my shoes.

I'm about to grab a few biscuits when I see a few items wrapped in parchment on the counter. I walk closer, suspicious of the items. However, there's writing on the parchment.

Good luck.

Tears threaten to make an appearance at the note. Blinking them away, I grab the parchment-wrapped items and a few biscuits and slip them into my bag. After placing my letter for Seamus on the counter, knowing Alan or Shannon will find it and know what to do, I take one final look around the kitchen before slipping out the garden door.

I warily make my way to the forest, hesitant to get too close. Last night really scared me, but there's only one way I'll get to the village unseen. If I want to have even the smallest chance of succeeding, I have to face it. Once I reach the top of the hill, the bushes begin to rustle, and I hold my breath at what could be hiding there.

"Caitria," Glac says. The grey rabbit hops through the bushes and stops right at the tree line. "Lady Cailleach said we would see you tonight."

"Are you leaving?" Sorcha asks, appearing next to Glac. The small white creature eyes my bag with a mixture of curiosity and sadness.

"Yes," I say. They're acting completely different from last night, like the dangers aren't here anymore. "Can you help me get to the village?"

"She told us you would need a horse," Glac says.

"A horse would be amazing," I remark with some relief. "Can you do that?"

"It's been so long since we've been a horse," Sorcha giggles before looking over at Glac. "Ready?"

Letting out a sigh, Glac hops into the forest with Sorcha following closely behind. I remain in place as I hear a series of loud cracks and pops. A strange burning smell permeates the air for a second before it dissipates. After a strange strangled neighing sound, a horse steps out of the forest, its eyes closed. It takes a few careful steps before nudging me with its snout.

I place a hand on its nose, noting the same scraggly yet soft fur that the rabbits have. The creature is covered in blobs of white and dark grey fur. I give it a few scratches, and it huffs before opening its eyes. I immediately notice four bright golden eyes. Before I can process it, the horse bows and tosses its head, waiting for me to get on its back. Not wanting to waste a second, I decide now isn't the time to focus on the strangeness of this and instead just climb up.

"Ready, Caitria?" the horse asks in an echoey, gravelly voice as it stands.

"I'm ready," I say, making sure to hold on to its mane as it begins to gallop toward the village.

The air rushes past my face as we go. The land around us looks distorted, and it feels like we've covered kilometers yet nothing at all. It feels like only a few seconds have passed before we arrive at the outskirts of the village. Another few seconds go by as the pucai trot among the alleys, making sure to stay in the light of the moon as much as possible. When we arrive at the side of the pub, the horse bows to let me off. I carefully get down as it stands back up.

"Farewell, Caitria," it says in a wavering voice, tears forming in its eyes. "You were our favorite, and we will never forget you."

"Thank you," I say, hugging its neck, "for everything."

Almost as soon as I let go, the horse bolts in the direction of the forest.

Every single light in the village is out, making the entire area seem very eerie. It's a stark contrast from how warm and welcoming it felt not long ago. I adjust my bag, making sure it's secured on my shoulder, before walking in the direction of the docks. Cormac didn't say where his boat was, so I silently hope I'm in the right place. I know he'll show up nearby soon enough, so I can follow him.

Though the village is clearly asleep, I decide not to risk being seen and crouch down near a holly bush. The branches rustle as they make space in the center of the plant, creating an opening for me to sit in.

Once I'm settled, it carefully closes around me, shielding me from the view of any passerby. The thorny leaves, so carefully angled away from me, move aside enough to allow me to see the start of the docks and most of the boardwalk next to the center of town.

As an icy breeze blows in from the water, and I shiver, thankful I had the foresight to wear warm clothes. With it being the start of winter, the weather is only going to get colder. A barely noticeable warmth seeps through my clothes as the shrub closes itself a little tighter around me to try and block me from the wind. I focus on the walkway in front of me and wait for the sound of footsteps, hoping it won't be too much longer. Illuminated by the light emanating from the thin sliver of the moon, the town looks almost like something out of a fairytale.

It doesn't take long before I hear the sound of footsteps in the distance. Anxiety immediately overtakes me as a thought enters my mind. While I waited for Cormac, I never stopped to think about whether anyone else might be out at this time. The sun isn't set to rise for at least another hour, but just because the isle is sleeping doesn't mean the people are. I tense up as they get closer and closer.

At the very least, I certainly wouldn't get an opportunity like this again. For all I know, Cormac might have told someone about our little conversation, and my plan might already be completely ruined. I take a deep breath to help calm myself as I focus on the path. The sound echoes in the stillness as a torchlight comes into view, a stark contrast to the rest of the village.

As it gets closer, I strain my eyes to see the face of the figure. It doesn't take long to realize that it won't be possible as the dark figure continues walking in the direction of the docks. The seconds pass slower than I ever thought possible as they get closer. I hold my breath as they pass by my hiding place.

While I don't see their face, there's only one person I know of who would wear such a knitted sweater. It's almost identical to the one Cormac wore that night in the pub. I wait for him to get a few yards away before the branches of the bush open up, letting me out. After silently thanking the plant, I rush after him. He doesn't make any sort of movement or sound that indicates that he is being followed.

When he walks right up to a large boat and climbs on, I attempt to follow suit. Unfortunately for me, I only make it past the rusty gate at the back of the boat when my bag falls from my grasp and makes an audible thud on the wooden deck. I cringe and look around frantically to see if anyone heard before rushing to the side of the small structure at the front end.

A quick peek through the window doesn't tell me much. The dirty glass is hard to see through, but from what I can tell, there isn't any light inside. There's no sound whatsoever, and I freeze. I watched the figure climb on this boat. Of that, I'm absolutely certain. However, there are no lights, and it's completely silent.

What if they found out? I think as a chill of terror trickles down my spine, my mind spiraling. *What if this is a trap?*

"Do you drink coffee?" a groggy voice asks. I look up and see Cormac standing there with two thermoses in hand.

"Sometimes, yes," I say with a nod and a massive sigh of relief. He hands me a thermos, taking a swig from his own.

"I was afraid I'd see ya today, Lady Caitria," he tells me.

I don't respond as he walks through the door into the small structure. It doesn't take me more than a second to follow him into the small covered seating area. At the front is the captain's area, complete with everything he needs to operate the boat. He turns on a single light as he gets the engine started. A low rumbling sound slowly gets louder as the boat comes to life.

Not knowing what to do or how I can help, I set my bag down on one of the benches nearby and take a seat. Once he's got the engine started, he walks over to me and sits across from me. Cormac leans back with a tired sigh. His eyes closed as he takes a sip from his thermos. After a second drink, he opens his eyes. They go wide for a brief moment. I don't even need to ask to know he's seen the scratches on my face.

"I take it the Lord and Lady Callihan don't know yer here?" he asks, clearing his throat, though it sounds more like a statement.

"No," I say as I touch the pendant that has since escaped its hiding place beneath my shirt. "And they'll never know," I say firmly. I watch as his eyes get a glazed look over them.

"They won't find out," he assures me. His immediate acceptance makes me wonder. "Are ya sure about this? You'd be leaving yer life here, and I'm guessing those marks on yer face'll be the least of yer worries if ya ever come back."

"I know," I quietly say as I look down at my hands, "but I have to do this."

He doesn't say anything for a while but lets out a grunt as he stands up and walks to the wheel.

"Very well," he tells me. "For what it's worth, ya would've made a great leader." He then sighs. "You're a smart young lady, and I'm proud to call myself one of yer people, if only for a little while longer."

"Thank you," I tell him as he pulls the boat away from the dock. The bumpiness of the water distracts me from the sight of Isle Draíocht shrinking away behind us.

"Get some rest, Lady Caitria," Cormac tells me after a minute. "I'll wake ya when we arrive."

It doesn't take long for the adrenaline to fade enough for me to fall asleep to the feeling of the waves. Though it only feels like a second, by the time Cormac wakes me up, we've arrived at the mainland.

"Do ya have a plan from here?" he asks with concern.

"Not really," I admit.

Getting away from the isle was hard enough, but as for having a plan after arriving at the mainland? I hadn't gotten much further than selling jewelry for money to try and find a place to stay.

"I see," he grumbles. He's silent for a moment before standing up. "Follow me."

He jumps off the boat, and not wanting to get left behind, I follow after him. He walks into the small town as I try to keep up. We pass more shops than I've ever seen in one place before. I look around in awe as we pass street light after street light, noticing the different signs and things in the windows. Bakeries, butchers, corner shops, and multiple clothing stores line the main street as we walk further into town. There's even a bookstore. It's dark as the sun hasn't begun to rise yet, but I can hardly imagine just how such a wondrous place would look with everything open and people wandering about.

We soon turn off the main street, walking through several brick-lined alleyways before he stops in front of a dark blue door. I glance up and see several windows, the curtains all drawn closed. Cormac knocks on the door and looks back at me with a small smile before the door swings open. On the other side of the threshold stands a woman a few years younger than him, her blonde hair thrown into a bun on the top of her head. Her thickly knitted sweater closely resembles his.

"Cormac!" she exclaims with joy as she pulls him in for a hug. He embraces her and lets her go with a smile. "Howya? Didn't think I'd see the likes of you today. What brings ya here?"

"Hiya, Claire. Look, I need a favor," he tells her as he gestures to me, her eyes going wide. "This is—"

"Cormac O'Shaughnessy!" the woman hisses as she smacks his arm before dragging him inside.

I follow closely behind, not wanting to be out in the open. She practically throws Cormac into the house before closing and latching the door behind me. She spares me a glance before closing her eyes and pinching the bridge of her nose.

"Tell me you didn't bring Caitria Callihan to my home," she says before looking directly at Cormac.

"Well, ya see," Cormac starts.

"Tell me," she demands, and I can see a frantic look in her eyes. "What is she doing here?"

"Claire, calm down," Cormac says as he reaches out to touch her arm.

"Do not. Tell me. To calm. Down," she snaps, pulling herself away from his touch. "I'm not an eejit. I know who she is."

"Excuse me," I try to say as the woman continues to seethe at Cormac.

"Ya didn't kidnap the poor lass. Did ya?" she exclaims, looking at me with wide eyes. "Poor thing looks absolutely shattered."

"Claire," Cormac scolds her. "What d'ya take me for?"

"Well, what am I supposed to think?" she shrieks. "Ya bring her here in the wee hours of the morning, on her wedding day, no less. Why the hell did ya bring her here, of all places? And why's her face marked up? Hell, why's she on the mainland?"

"Hey, now, if you would just let me—" Cormac begins, raising his voice.

"I asked him to help," I say in a louder voice than intended. They both turn to look at me, going silent. "Sorry, but I had no choice." I reach up to touch my pendant again. "I can leave, but you've got to keep my being here a secret."

Their eyes both glaze over for a second before clearing. I feel bad about using the pendant for such things, but I know it's for the best. If Mother or Father found out, I'd be dragged back there against my will.

"What'd ya mean?" the woman asks, gesturing for me to sit on the couch behind me.

"It's complicated," I say slowly, thankful they're no longer attacking each other. "But you've got to know I have good reasons." I open my mouth to say something else but feel myself getting choked up. "I understand if you can't help me, but please, at least don't tell anyone you saw me."

Sympathy crosses the woman's eyes as she looks at Cormac. They share a look and she sighs. "I'll do what I can, but ya have to leave quickly. Most of us know about the things that go on at Isle Draíocht, and yer wedding to the McNeillain boy is something everyone knows is going on."

I nod and feel a wave of relief. She looks at Cormac and lets out yet another sigh, giving him a small nod.

"Saoirise, our sister, lives just outside Dublin," Cormac says. "She runs a youth hostel there and is always looking for help. Claire'll call ahead and let her know you're coming."

They both share some additional details about Saoirise before Claire steps out of the room to make the phone call. We all agreed that Cormac has to get back as soon as possible, so after saying a very brief goodbye, he leaves to head back to Isle Draíocht.

"Are ya sure you want to do this, Lady Caitria?" Claire asks as we get to the bus station less than a half-hour later.

"I've never been more sure about anything," I tell her. "Thank you for your help."

"Think nothing of it, dearie," she says quietly. "I hope ya find what you're looking for."

"I hope so, too," I reply with a smile as I walk up the stairs and into the bus. She stands on the curb, waving at me as the bus begins to pull away from the station.

Never in my wildest dreams did I ever think this would actually work. But it did, and I know once I get to Dublin, Saoirise O'Shaughnessy will be there waiting for me.

Chapter 17

The bus ride takes a lot longer than expected. We pass villages and towns much larger than what I am used to. Cars pass us as we go along down the road. At each and every stop, people get on and off the bus, and every single time, without fail, I feel like I can't breathe until we're moving once again. The sun rises after the third stop, and I realize that everyone on the isle must've found their letters by now. Or if they haven't found them yet, they soon will.

Thinking about Enya reading my letter brings tears to my eyes. I turn completely toward the window and am thankful only about ten people are on the bus at any one time. No one pays me any attention. I see it in my mind so clearly how frantic Mother must be as she unlocks my door to find my letter.

I can practically see her face going bright red with rage as she tells Brigit. The argument that has no doubt ensued between them from my disappearance must be booming throughout the manor. Father must know by now and is likely instructing Alan to search the isle for me. They must be trying to keep this news secret, but eventually, they'll have to tell the people there won't be a wedding.

Poor Enya is likely all alone in this. I hope that she's at least gone to Shannon for some comfort. She must be trying so hard to keep it together, just like she always does. The only solace I have is that she has Shannon.

My mind then goes to Seamus. I have no idea how he will react to this news, but I know he will no doubt be questioned. I only hope Alan is able to get my letter to him and that he isn't angry or hurt by my leaving.

Eventually, we reach the final stop. I climb down the stairs at the brick station. The few windows of the building look out at the different covered stops. A cold rain starts to sprinkle down as I approach the side of the building. Claire said her sister Saoirise would be waiting for me here. She showed me a photo of the curvy blonde woman a few years younger than her before I got on the bus, letting me know to look for her in a scarf in all shades of green when I arrived. However, the more I look around, no one fits that description.

I clutch my bag a bit closer as a few people pass by in all different directions. It's overwhelming to be around so many people, and I find myself standing directly against the brick wall of the building. The metal rafters protect me from the rain as I look around. A concrete curb knocks against my ankles as I press myself against the wall. I take a step up to see if I can get a better look around the station.

People begin to clear out a little as two buses further down take off, and my stomach sinks. Very few people remain in the station. Tears begin to form as I realize she might not come. The rain picks up as I feel the first few tears begin to fall. My breathing picks up, and the floodgates open. I try to control my breathing and get it under control, but as I wipe my eyes against the scratchy arm of my sweater, the reality of the situation hits me.

How stupid am I to have thought this would actually work? I internally scold myself.

Placing my bag at my feet, I try to figure out what my next step will be, but I don't even know where to start. I don't know anyone here, and I have no money to pay for a bus fare. Even if I did, I wouldn't even know where to go. I can't possibly do anything right now. A recognizable red structure nearby houses a phone, but even if I had the coins to pay for it, I wouldn't even have a number to dial.

"Cait!" a woman's voice calls out.

I glance in the direction of the voice and see a woman a little older than Shannon walking toward me. She's bundled up in a flannel with a colorful scarf wrapped around her neck. The black umbrella she carries overhead protects her short blonde hair from the rain. Now standing in front of me, she flings her arms around me and pulls me in for a hug.

"I'm so glad yer here!" she tells me in an excited voice. I hug her back after a brief moment of surprise. "Let's grab yer bags before we go, yeah?"

"I've got it," I tell her as I place my bag over my shoulder, holding onto it tightly. She gives me a puzzled look but doesn't say anything.

"Grand," she says before turning around abruptly as she walks away from the buses. "Follow me!"

I follow along behind her, taking care not to get lost in the crowds of people starting to gather all across the station. Between the noise and the business, I feel very overwhelmed. I also feel a prickling on the back of my neck, as if I am being watched. While I want to look around to see if anyone is, in fact, watching me, I know I'd so easily lose Saoirise in the crowd. I speed up as I try to keep up with her while she walks toward a small car. She slaps the top and gives me a wide smile.

"This, here, is our lovely ride!" she tells me with a chuckle. "Toss yer bag in the back, and we will be right on our way."

I do as I am told as she starts up the car, encouraging it to sputter to life. Buildings pass by outside, and I watch with awe. I knew the isle was isolated, but I'm only now realizing just how different life is elsewhere. The tallest buildings on the isle only have two floors. It never occurred to me that buildings could be taller than that. That such a place could exist is beyond anything I could've dreamed. The brightly lit signs and shops are just starting to open up and start their days as we pass by.

Soon, we're well on our way outside of Dublin. The scenery shifts abruptly from shops to rows and rows of tall, narrow houses. The occasional tree is planted, and as we drive past, each one looks like it stands up a little taller. It feels almost welcoming. I watch out of the window as we get further and further away from the city center.

"So, Cait," she says after we're on the main road. "Cormac didn't tell me much, but I remember the isle well enough to know that the sneaky bastard lied to me about ya."

I feel my face go pale. Claire wanted to tell Saoirise who I am, but Cormac made her swear to tell her a lie. She refused, so Cormac called her. Clearly, Saoirise knows well enough that I'm not just the daughter of a friend looking for a place to stay.

"Now, I won't ask questions, but I need to know if *they* know or if I might be expecting any unwanted visitors," she tells me.

"They're probably just finding out," I tell her honestly. "I don't know whether they'll come looking or not. To be honest, I don't plan to stick around long enough for them to find me."

"So what's yer plan?" she asks as she glances at me out of the corner of her eye. "Ya can't expect them to not come looking for ya, and I am guessing they didn't exactly give you any money."

"I've got some jewelry I can sell," I tell her, and she chuckles at that.

"Are we talking anything nice, or just that stuff yer gran wore?" she asks.

"It's a few birthday gifts," I tell her, cringing at the sound of it. "There are also a few things I was given as wedding presents."

"Ah, lovely," she says as she looks around. The lack of traffic allows her to turn down a narrow road without much of a pause. "Look, I know a lad. He'll help ya get a good price, but it probably won't be much. Have ya got any other plans?"

"No, but Cormac said you might need help around the hostel?" I say with a hopeful voice. "I can help out."

"Not a bad idea," she tells me after pondering it for a second. "But ya need to keep a low profile, yeah? I can't afford to have any problems. If ya help out and pull yer weight, ya can stay there, and I'll pay you well. It won't be easy, though."

"Yes," I tell her with a relieved sigh. I had half expected her to laugh, especially since I've never worked a day in my life. "Thank you so much, Saoirise."

"Yeah, yeah," she says in response as we turn down another road. "Just don't think I'll go easy on ya, *Lady Caitria*."

"I'd expect nothing less," I tell her, laughing nervously at hearing my title. "I'm looking for a fresh start. From now on, I'm just Cait."

We soon arrive at the hostel. The building is along a long row of other identical buildings yet is distinguishable from the others by the bright blue door and weather-faded hanging sign, *O'Shaughnessy's Youth Hostel*, indicating to passersby that beyond the door lies a place for young travelers. I can practically hear water against the shoreline as we get out of the car. I glance further down the road and see the water in the distance.

A smile forms on my face at the sight. I take a deep breath in as a frigid gust of air whips across my face. It stings as I suppress a shiver. Saoirise opens the door, and we go inside to escape from the cold winter morning. We enter a short hallway with a locked door at the opposite end. A counter with a window carved out of the wall sits on one side. A wave of warm air greets us as we go past the locked door into the building. She gives me a brief tour, pointing out the room attached to the window in the hallway.

"Yer going to be spending a few hours a day there," she tells me as we walk. "It's where they'll check in and out. Ya might also get a few asking for directions or recommendations. We've got a list for that written down in there for ya."

Walking further into the building, Saoirise points out the staircase to the rooms and the bathrooms before stopping to unlock a plain wooden door. It creaks as it opens. She flicks on the light as we walk inside.

"Welcome home," she says as she gives me a moment to take in the space.

It's a cozy room with a single bed, a desk and chair, and a few shelves for clothes. There's a narrow door near the front of the room. I open it to find a small bathroom with just enough space for a sink, a toilet, and a shower. It's quite a bit smaller than what I had at the manor, but it feels much warmer and more welcoming than my bedroom ever did. I drop my bag and take a deep breath.

It's a blank space, but there's something so exciting about it. For the first time since I left the isle, I finally feel like this could actually work. This is just a stop on the way to somewhere else, but I feel a hopefulness peeking out from a wall of fear. Maybe, just maybe, they won't find me. Nerves and excitement flow through me as I begin to see the possibilities unfolding.

She gives me another second to take it in before continuing with the tour of the building. Several of the young people staying there are slowly starting their days as we walk around. Overall, it's not a large place, and as soon as she helps me make a cup of tea and shows me where the scones are for a quick breakfast, laughter begins to fill the halls and trickle down from the two floors above.

While my heart aches for those I left behind, I feel myself smiling at this new beginning. That ray of hope gets a little bit brighter as I'm finally starting to see a future away from the isle. Somehow, I know I made the right choice in leaving and, hopefully, this will be the start of a beautiful new beginning for everyone.

Chapter 18

The man Saoirise mentioned would buy my jewelry owns a pawn shop a few doors down the street. She took me there that afternoon on my first day, warning me to keep quiet and let her do all the talking. After he had inspected each necklace, bracelet, and earring carefully, he gave me a cautious look.

"Where'd ya get 'em?" he had asked in a strong accent, eyeing me up and down skeptically. "Ya didn' steal 'em, yeah?"

"Course she didn' steal 'em," Saoirise replied. "Does she look like a thief?"

"I always gotta ask, Saoirise," the man said with a sigh. "I take it she don' wanna be connected to 'em?"

"No," she told him.

"Oof, alrigh'," He mumbled before placing them back in a cloth bag Saoirise had given me and pushing it toward me. "Come 'ere in a couple a days, yeah? Gonna need time to get 'em clean."

Saoirise promised me that he'd make sure they were untraceable once he had finished drafting up some sort of paperwork for them.

She showed me around the town a bit, pointing out a pub, a few small restaurants, and other shops that sold a variety of things, from clothing and household items to books and plants. That last shop was by far my favorite. As we walked past, it was almost like I could actually feel the plants stretching and saying hello.

It's been a few days since then, and I haven't had a chance to go back. Saoirise kept her promise in giving me work, and as she said, it's far from easy at times. However, something in it is satisfying. Over the past few days, I've settled into a routine. Early in the morning, I get a cup of coffee and a small pastry from the communal kitchen before going to the front desk and relieving the overnight person. Some mornings, I help people check in or out.

Saoirise invited me to join her at the pub for lunch today. I'm looking forward to it, especially since most of my days after work are spent either sitting near the water or reading all sorts of things to learn about the world outside the isle. I've just opened a book Saoirise recommended when I hear someone clear their throat.

I look up to find a young woman. Her dirty blonde hair is tied up in a bun at the top of her head. Though it's freezing outside, she's only sporting a flannel to keep her warm. She pushes her reflective wire-framed sunglasses up, revealing bright green eyes.

"Hey," she says as she leans against the counter with a smile. "Does this place have a bed open? I just got in and could seriously use a nap and a shower."

"Yes," I tell her as I flip through the room log. "We've got an opening in Room 4G. It'll just be you. The other girl checked out yesterday."

"Oh, perfect," she says with a sigh of relief. "You can't imagine how crazy my day's been. This just made it so much better."

"How long'll you be staying?" I ask her with a smile.

"I dunno." She laughs. "My flight home isn't for another week, so probably until then."

"Got it," I reply as I make a note of that before giving her a key. "It'll be ten pounds a night, so it'll be seventy pounds. Is that all right?"

"Yup, that should be fine," she replies as she digs through her wallet. "Do I need to pay it all now or when I leave?"

"It's half now and half when you check out," I tell her as she hands me a handful of banknotes and coins. After counting them up, I unlock the door to the building and let her in.

There's an easy-going feeling to her. She tells me about her travels as we walk up the stairs. Her animated story about her morning has me laughing by the time we reach the top of the stairs. By the time we get to the fourth floor, I feel completely at ease talking with her.

"I'm Anna, by the way," she says as I show her to her room.

"I'm Cait," I tell her as we come to Room 4G. "This is where you'll be staying."

"Great, thanks," she tells me with a smile. "Say, when do you get off? Wanna go to the beach later?"

"I'm meeting a friend for lunch after I'm off," I tell her. "Maybe later?"

"You bet," Anna replies as she unlocks the door to her room. "I'm going to get some sleep, so I'll see you around."

"Sleep well," I tell her before heading back to the front desk.

What if she was sent by Mother and Father? I think as soon as I sit down.

Anna was extremely nice, and I could tell that we would be great friends. While unlikely, I can't shake the thought that she might've been sent by someone on the isle. Her accent was very clearly American, and she didn't mention being part Irish or anything like a lot of the people staying here. No matter how much I want to push that thought away and write it off as part of an overactive imagination, I know I can't be too cautious.

Picking my book back up, I try to focus on the words, only to fail miserably. Thankfully, there are only two checkouts before my shift ends. I hand the desk off to the next person before stopping by my room. I throw on a thick sweater and a jacket before walking down the street to the pub.

As soon as I step inside, I see Saoirise sitting at the bar. I hang my jacket on the coat rack and watch as she talks with a bartender who's probably a few years older than her. His dark hair falls across his eyes as they talk. Something in the way he smiles at her makes me think that they're a bit more than having a friendly conversation. Their conversation abruptly stops as Saoirise looks my way, waving me over.

"Howya?" she asks, giving me a quick hug before I sit on the stool next to hers.

"Grand. You?" I reply as the bartender brings me a small, hand-written menu. Before I can look at anything, Saoirise waves it away.

"Two butcher's plates," she tells him.

"On it," he replies, tapping the bar twice before walking away.

"So," she says, turning toward me. "How're ya liking working?"

"It's good," I tell her honestly. "I've missed out on so much, so it's been grand meeting so many people."

"Glad ya feel that way," she replies with a smile. "Now, I've been chatting with Tom here, and he said he's in need of someone to help out with the midday rush. Think ya'd be interested?"

"Ya can say no," the bartender says as he brings over two plates of food. "Saoirise said yer a hard worker and looking for some cash. I'd pay ya fairly, and I won't expect ya to stay forever. I just need someone to help while my usual lass is traveling for the holidays."

"Why don't ya think on it over some food and let Tom know before we leave?" Saoirise suggests.

I nod in response as we dig in. Tom walks over to help out a few other patrons who've come in for an early lunch. Saoirise and I don't talk much as we eat. It's mainly mundane things, like the weather and whatnot. After a few minutes, I bring up Anna, trying to be discreet about my concerns.

"She's American?" Saoirise asks between bites.

"Yeah," I reply, taking a sip of water. "I'm a little worried."

"Ah," she replies, catching my unspoken question. "I'll keep an eye out, but ya said she just got in today, so I wouldn't worry."

I nod in response as we continue with our lunch. One of the things I've come to learn about Saoirise is that she won't probe me about anything. She probably knows more than she lets on, but she keeps it to herself and never pushes me to talk about things.

Soon, we're done eating, and Tom comes back over. He brushes his dark hair out of his face before wiping his hands on the towel resting on his shoulder.

"How was it?" he asks, removing our plates.

"Grand," I reply with a smile.

"Good enough to take the job?" he asks hopefully, and Saoirise and I laugh in response.

"I'd have a few days off and most nights, right?" I ask, trying to negotiate.

"Of course." He laughs and then reaches his hand out toward me. "So? Ya joining us for a bit?"

"I'd love to," I reply, shaking his hand.

We leave shortly after that. Saoirise makes sure I get all the necessary details before we go. She hurries back to the hostel and out of the cold while I make a stop at the beach. I perch on a bench at the edge of the narrow boardwalk and take a deep breath, listening to the sound of the water. Closing my eyes for a minute, I let the sounds calm me.

I can feel the sun shining down, and even in the wintery chill, it warms my face ever so slightly. I wrap my jacket a little tighter around me as the chill begins to seep into my bones. The seagulls caw all around me, but after a moment, the sounds fade. The warmth fades away, and an ominous feeling comes over me. I open my eyes and find the clouds rolling in. What was a sunny winter afternoon is now gone, replaced with dark grey storm clouds.

My skin pricks, but I quickly realize it's not from the cold. I look toward the water and don't see anything. However, in the blink of an eye, a young man appears and begins walking toward me. Even though it's cloudy, I instantly recognize him as the one of Carman's sons.

He gives me a smile that sends chills down my spine as he gets closer and closer. I'm frozen in place, remembering that dream all too vividly. For a moment, I fear that I've fallen asleep, but the wind blowing my hair across my face is biting. Dreams don't have that. The closer he gets, the more I feel my pulse quicken in fear.

He's so close now that I can see the darkness in his red eyes when he stops in his tracks. He reaches a hand toward me, and I can see the scars scattered across it. Dain stalks toward me, getting closer and closer with each passing second. I want to run far away from his reach, but I can't move my legs. Suddenly, his smile fades and goes stoic as he lowers his arm. When I feel a hand on my shoulder, I jump around and shriek.

"Oh, Cait, I'm so sorry," Anna says. "I just saw you sitting there and thought you might want some company. I didn't mean to scare you."

"It's all right," I tell her, looking over my shoulder at Dain. He looks enraged at the interruption but remains silent.

"Do you know him?" Anna asks quietly.

"Yes," I say without thinking. "We should leave. Now."

"Good idea," she replies quietly, looping her arm through mine. "I noticed a few card games. Wanna play one when we get back?"

"That sounds grand," I tell her as we hurry away.

I look behind me a few times as we hurry back to the hostel. Dain doesn't follow us and remains in the same spot near the boardwalk that we left. I can practically hear his voice in my head. *You won't be so lucky next time*, it says.

I'm so distracted that it takes me a moment longer than normal to unlock the inner door after we get to the hallway inside the hostel entrance. As soon as we're safely inside, Anna drags me into the kitchen, sitting me down at one of the small tables. She doesn't say anything as she pours two cups of tea, bringing them back to the table before looking at me.

"Did he give you those?" she asks bluntly, pointing at the fading scratches on my face. "He looked like he wanted to hurt you."

"What?" I ask, momentarily confused. "Oh, yes," I warn her. "If you see him again, you need to get as far away as possible. He's very dangerous."

"Of course," she tells me, grabbing my hands. "I will if you will. No freezing, okay?"

"Okay," I tell her with a relieved sigh.

"I'm here if you ever want to talk about it," Anna says softly after a minute.

"Thank you," I reply.

We sip our tea quietly. She doesn't ask any questions after that. For some reason, I don't feel so alone anymore. While she's practically a stranger, her being here and being open to listening brings some comfort.

Chapter 19

A few days pass after seeing Dain at the beach. I'm more on edge than before as I'm not only worried about people from the isle coming to look for me but Carman and her sons. One of my few comforts has been the flowers Saoirise insists we keep at the front desk. There are only a few plants in total, but during the slower times, I try to see just how much I can interact with them. They're usually bright and colorful whenever I walk into the room each and every morning. Every now and then, their aroma will fill the room, particularly when I'm overly anxious. I've even found that the plants will reach toward me, though I've only gotten that reaction once.

Outside of my work, my nerves get the better of me, especially whenever I need to go out by myself. Much to my surprise, however, that rarely happens. Whenever I finish my morning shift at the hostel, Saoirise is usually on her way out. It's typically to run to the store to pick up random odds and ends for the hostel or to meet friends for lunch. Regardless, she usually walks with me down to the pub before going on her way.

After work, I usually see Anna making her way down the street. The more time we spend together, the more it feels like we've been friends my entire life. We get along so well, and any suspicion I had about her disappeared shortly after she helped me get away from Dain. We've started getting dinner together and wandering around town. Tonight, we go to the pawn shop after dinner.

Anna looks around the shop while the man talks with me in the small back office. It's piled high with various papers and goods. Saoirise negotiated a good price for my things over the past few days, so all I need to do is drop them off and pick up the money.

"I didn' see ya, and ya never came 'ere, yeah?" he grumbles to me as he inspects the jewelry one last time before locking them away in a large safe on the floor.

"Of course," I tell him as he hands me a thick envelope.

It only takes a few minutes for me to finish trading my goods and making sure he gave me the amount he and Saoirise agreed on. Afterward, Anna and I begin walking down the street when I see a familiar face that stops me in my tracks. A tall, slender man with dark red hair and glasses is looking in shop windows. While his face is hard to see in the shadows, a lamp near one of the shop doors illuminates it enough that my suspicions are confirmed. That's the same man I bumped into at the pub on the isle.

He hasn't seen us as he continues peeking into shop windows, clearly searching for something. Or, in this case, someone. In one hand, he holds a piece of paper. We're far enough away that I can't see what's on the paper, but I can guess. Panic instantly sets in.

My pulse races and my mind spins. A chill runs down my spine as my hands get clammy. I try to stay calm as I duck into the nearest side street. The shaking in my legs doesn't help as I wring my gloved hands together. Anna follows after me as I try to keep my head down and try not to draw attention to myself.

"Where are we going?" she asks. "This place is kinda creepy, Cait."

"Sorry, but can you keep your voice down?" I ask quietly, hurrying down the street.

"What's wrong?" Anna asks as she notices my shift in demeanor. "Did you see that guy from the beach again?"

"No," I tell her as we keep walking, still wringing my hands to try and keep them from shaking. "It's just someone from back home."

"Wait. Shouldn't you go say hello?" she suggests, but I shake my head in response.

"No, I really shouldn't," I tell her. "In fact, it's best that he doesn't know I'm here."

I can't believe they managed to find me so quickly. I've barely been here a week. While I don't know his name, I'm absolutely certain I've seen that man before at numerous events on the isle. The fact that he's here can't mean anything good.

He's the port master's nephew. During the day, he's a butcher. However, he's been known to help out whenever someone needs help. In a way, he's like an unofficial detective of the isle. The fact that he's here tells me more than enough.

We walk in silence for a few minutes, hurrying down unlit streets toward the safety of the hostel. I do my best to move as quickly and quietly as possible. Anna, on the other hand, tries to keep up, puffs of clouds forming as she huffs.

"So, Cait." She huffs after we turn down another side street. "What's your story?"

"What do you mean?" I ask, checking behind us to see if we've been followed.

"I mean, what's your story," she explains as we slow down enough for her to catch her breath. "Like, you know mine. I grew up in the United States and came here for an adventure after ending things with my boyfriend. So what about you?"

"Ah, well," I say, trying not to reveal too much. I check over my shoulder and let out a sigh of relief as the street behind us remains empty. "I grew up in Ireland, kind of in the middle of nowhere, and I left home, and now I'm here."

"Why'd you leave home?" she asks as she dodges a questionable pile of trash on the street.

"I needed a change," I tell her, not exactly lying.

"I gotcha," she responds. "What're you gonna do next?"

"Honestly," I say with a heavy sigh. "I'm not quite sure. I'll need to move on soon."

I wouldn't even know where to go, but I'm not sure anywhere is far away enough, I think. We walk in silence until we get back to the main street.

"Where're you going to go?" Anna ponders.

"I've no idea," I say with a laugh as I look around to make sure we're still in the clear. "I haven't quite gotten that far."

"Well, that's not good. Have you ever thought about leaving Ireland?" she asks with a laugh, placing her hands on her hips.

"Where would I go, though?" I say, more to myself than anything as we arrive at the hostel. "I came here because I had someone here who could help. I don't know anywhere else to go."

"You could always come with me," she suggests, shrugging her shoulders. A smile forms on her face, and it's clear this was just a passing thought, but she's already set on the idea. "I'd have to ask my parents, but I'm sure you'd be able to stay for a bit while you figure out your next move."

Anna pauses her thoughts for a moment while I quickly unlock the hostel door so we can get safely inside, away from the cold and unwelcome visitors. When we get to the kitchen, I turn to see that she's smiling even wider.

"Mom and Dad could always use help at their cafe, too, so we could work together, too," Anna says before clapping her hands together and letting out an excited squeal. "Cait, we could be roommates. Or, I guess you could stay at Gran's old place."

As she continues talking, I can imagine it so clearly. Even when around Enya or Seamus, or even Shannon, I never felt like I could be myself. For the first time in my life, maybe I could have an actual friend and live my life the way I want. Maybe I could even explore this connection the Cailleach talked about. The plants at the front desk come to mind, and I imagine myself living completely surrounded by plants.

As the possibilities bloom in my mind, I feel a smile forming on my face as I munch on a chocolate biscuit I pulled down from a cabinet. I give myself another second to think about it before forcing it from my mind. It's a future I hesitate to think about too much. Such a thing would be a dream, but it's just that. An impossible dream. There's probably no way it could actually happen.

"At the very least, you'd be able to get away from whatever you're running from," she says before her smile falls. "I don't mean to force this on you. But just think, you could get away and hide out from whatever you're hiding from."

I pause at those words, remembering something the Cailleach told me. *You'll know where to go.*

Would it be too much to hope this could be my life? I think. Maybe, just maybe, I'm meant to go with Anna. Barely a month ago, I was convinced that I'd spend my entire life being Lady Callihan. Now, I've not only run away from an arranged marriage, but I managed to escape the isle. Perhaps it's time to start having those impossible dreams.

"In the meantime, though, we'll need to change up your look," Anna tells me, a smile once again forming on her face as she lightly touches my hair and the sleeve of my sweater. "Your hair is so pretty, but I know it's you from a mile away. And your clothes are kinda older looking. If we change up your hair and some of your clothes, maybe they won't find you as easily?"

"What'd you have in mind?" I ask, feeling a wave of nervousness and excitement.

"Hey, Saoirise," she yells as she rushes down the hallway toward the front desk. Anna knocks at the door to the front desk. "Got any scissors?"

"Why do ya need those?" Saoirise says, cracking the door open and popping her head out.

"Cait needs a haircut," she says, grinning at me. "Wanna help?"

"You sure?" Saoirise asks, looking pointedly at me while opening the door wider.

I nod and she must see something in my eyes because she calls out to the other person working the desk to take over. She grabs a pair of scissors, handing them to Anna, and gestures toward the bathroom in her room.

"Can ya bring a chair and a towel?" she asks her, opening the door for me. "Cait and I will be there in a sec."

"Got it," Anna excitedly exclaims as she walks off.

"Ya good?" Saoirise asks, placing both hands on my shoulders.

The fear from earlier comes back with a force, and I feel myself begin to tremble. Tears begin to form even as I try to blink them away. It's like all my hope shattered the instant I saw that man. Now that I'm in a safe spot, it's like I can't push my fears and emotions aside, and I start to cry. Saoirise immediately pulls me into a hug, stroking my hair.

"You're all right," Saoirise softly says as she pulls me in for a hug as I sob. "What happened?"

"They're here," I mumble into her shoulder. "I can't believe they found me. I saw him looking in the windows. They must've sent him to bring me back."

"I don't know his name," I say with a sniffle. "But I know why he's here. I saw him looking in windows, and I just know he's here for me."

"Shite," she mumbles under her breath. "How'd they get here so quickly?"

"What am I going to do?" I ask her as she pulls away. I feel myself spiraling as I begin to hyperventilate. "I don't have enough money. I can't leave. They're going to take me back. I can't go back."

"Cait. Look at me," she tells me, grabbing my chin and forcing me to look at her. "Ya won't be going back. They won't find ya. Do ya hear me?"

I nod, trying to take deep breaths in an attempt to calm down. I close my eyes, wiping away a few stray tears. It takes a few seconds, but I eventually get my breathing slowed down.

"Anna had the right idea about changing yer hair," Saoirise says. "We'll cut it a bit, and ya can borrow some clothes. I'll talk with Tom and let him know ya can't help in the front. Ya can help with cleaning around here."

"Okay, okay," I say as I process what she says.

"Ya can't stay here, though," she tells me. "Do ya have a plan?"

"No, but—" I start before we hear someone clearing their throat behind us.

"She can come with me," Anna says, dragging a chair in behind her. "She'll need a plane ticket and a passport, but she can come with me."

"Ya sure?" Saoirise asks her as I take a seat in the chair, now positioned in the center of the small bathroom.

"Absolutely," Anna replies, securing a towel around my neck with a hair tie. "I mean, I'll make sure it's all right with my parents tomorrow, but it shouldn't be a problem."

"Grand," Saoirise mumbles as she takes the scissors from Anna.

After identifying how short to cut my hair, I close my eyes as I feel the first cut. My hair, which has always hung halfway down my back, is now going to sit right above my shoulders. Saoirise cuts it skillfully as Anna watches on. I hear them talking, but it feels so far away. I feel like I'm in shock as I can't quite focus on anything.

Once the cut is complete and they're thoroughly pleased with it, I go back to my room and lie down. My mind spins at everything that's happened in the past few hours. The nerves come back as my hands begin to shake again. They must've noticed as they talk softly, bringing some of Saoirise's clothes to my room.

After the last few pieces of clothes are in, Saoirise leaves, saying something about checking in a bit later. Anna helps me get under the blankets. Once she's sure I'm tucked in, she pulls the rolling cot out from under my bed. She turns out the lights and lies down next to me. Reaching over, she grabs my hand and gives it a comforting squeeze.

"Let me know if you need anything, all right?" she asks. I nod silently in response, knowing she can't see me. Anna gives my hand another light squeeze before letting it go. I send a silent thanks to the Cailleach for working whatever magic she did to bring my best friend to me.

"I'll call my parents tomorrow morning," she tells me after a few minutes. I close my eyes as she starts telling me all sorts of things about where she lives. Before I know it, I'm falling asleep.

Chapter 20

True to her word, Anna used the phone at the hostel to call home the morning after cutting my hair. She made me stay nearby just in case they asked to talk with me, so I stayed silent and watched. A combination of fear and anxiety made me unable to stand completely still. I fidgeted with my hands the entire time, expecting them to start yelling or threatening her as soon as she asked. However, that never happened.

When they answered the phone, she started chatting away like she was talking with a friend. It was so different from what I knew that I could hardly believe she was talking with her parents. Almost as soon as she mentioned me, they immediately suggested I come to stay with them. She didn't even need to ask. I could practically hear their excitement through the phone at meeting a new friend of Anna's. It warmed my heart and replaced all my misgivings with excitement and hope.

It's been two days since then, and we've been talking more and more about our plans. Tom at the pub said the red-haired man left shortly after arriving. Apparently, he'd been showing my picture to anyone who would listen, but no one gave me away. It warmed my heart hearing these people who hardly know me are willing to help me hide away. However, I know I'll have to move on soon before they send anyone else.

My new shorter hair takes some time to get used to. Most people seem to like it, and the more times goes by, the more I start to agree with them. Something is freeing about not having to tie it back all the time. Saoirise's clothes, on the other hand, take me a bit longer to adjust to.

"I think you look great," Anna tells me after work tonight. "Your clothes never fit you quite right."

"You're right," I relent as we walk back from the pub. "They still feel strange, though."

"Of course they do." She laughs. "It's cause they're the right size. Don't worry, though. Mom and I will take you shopping after we get there."

I smile at the thought. A gust of wind blows down the street and I shiver. I pull the borrowed flannel tighter around me. Burying half of my face in the dark grey scarf, I silently decide that scarves may be part of my new wardrobe.

"It's colder than normal," Anna comments after a minute, pulling me from my new fascination. "You feel it, too, right? It's not just me?"

"It's pretty cold," I say in agreement, my breath creating a small cloud in front of me.

The street lights, while few and far between, seem dimmer than normal as well. One flickers in the distance before going out. The moon is completely covered by the clouds overhead. The eerie feeling only grows as another street light flickers. An ominous feeling creeps in as I notice a particularly thick fog forming around our feet.

My palms feel clammy, but I try to ignore it, focusing on getting inside as fast as possible. Another street light goes out. I can see the red door of the hostel, but it feels like it's getting farther away the closer we get. Panic begins to set in. A wave of dizziness flows over me as the back of my neck tingles. It's so strong that I can't ignore it. I'm instantly on high alert. It's almost like we're being watched.

I stop walking and whip my head around, but I don't see anything. The buildings around us grow dim as another street light goes out. It almost feels like we're caged in as the shadows get closer. My heart pounds in my chest and my stomach drops. This scene feels all too familiar. I realize too late that we should've run away when we had the chance. The blood drains from my face as I watch the fog begin to rise and take the shape of a woman.

"What the hell is that?" Anna asks in a low voice.

I don't even look over. I know she's looking at the same thing.

"Run," I tell her as quietly as I can.

As soon as the word leaves my mouth, the banshee gives us a grotesque smile, her sharp teeth on full display.

"Hello again," she says in the same horrible voice as she reaches her arm toward us. She lets out a bloodcurdling scream as she begins to drift toward us.

Anna covers her ears and doubles over. I lean over and grab one of her arms. She looks at me, and I begin to help her move away. We barely make it a few steps when the banshee rushes at us.

"Not so fast, little human," she taunts as she stops right in front of my face.

Up close, I can see a black ooze seeping through her teeth. The stench of rotting fish fills my nose, and I almost gag at the scent. Anna's screams sound so far away. She stumbles forward, vomiting to the side as a cold sweat begins to cover her skin. I try to help her stand up as the banshee moves a strand of hair away from my face. Her claw-like fingertips almost graze my skin as her horrifying smile only grows.

"No!" I scream as she laughs, reaching a hand toward my face.

I feel Anna slip, and I make sure I have a good grip on her arm so she doesn't fall. She's trembling, and tears stream down her face as she keeps covering her ears. The banshee screeches again, and I almost trip over my own feet as dizziness and nausea shoot through me, accompanied by a sharp pain in my head. My breathing speeds up as a cold sweat soaks my shirt. My vision begins to blur as I remain standing. I place a hand on my chest as my heart begins to throb.

"Leave!" I shout as I feel my legs weaken and begin shaking.

The banshee stops moving. I try to remain standing, shocked to see it rooted in place. Fear courses through me as she stays there, glaring at me with her black eyes before slowly sinking down into the fog. I'm frozen as I try to process what just happened.

As soon as I realize she's actually gone, I make sure Anna can stand before pulling her the rest of the way to the hostel. I don't hesitate as I throw open the door and slam it closed behind us. I don't let go of Anna as I unlock the second door. It closes behind us, and setting Anna to the ground, I make sure to lock it behind us.

Wasting no time, I help her up and into my room down the hallway. I prop her up against the toilet before rummaging through my bag to find the tea Shannon gave me. I don't have many, but I manage to find one at the bottom of the bag. I stumble into the bathroom to fill my small electric kettle with water. I dump the tea in as I start it. The wait for the water to boil feels like it takes an eternity.

My legs give out underneath me, and I fall to the floor. I drag myself over to Anna as she goes pale, sweat covering her skin. She begins to shiver, and I tear off the flannel and scarf I was wearing. I wrap it around her the best I can before I begin to sway. My vision begins to blur, but I try to keep my senses.

I try to stand and manage to stumble over to the kettle. A sip of the bitter liquid straight from the spout tells me it's barely warm. While I know it needs more time, I can't wait on it. Taking another sip, I manage to bring it over to Anna. She's barely able to open her eyes, but she opens her mouth slightly and takes a sip of the liquid. As soon as a few drops get in her mouth, she coughs and spits it out.

"D-drink," I stutter as I try to focus.

She nods and takes a drink. Her face contorts at the taste, but she swallows it. I help her sit up a little more, just enough for another sip. She takes another and another with little prompting. After she's gotten a bit more down, the color slowly starts coming back as she stops shivering.

I feel a short-lived wave of relief as I take a huge gulp of the liquid, choking it down. My vision fades as the kettle slips through my fingers. I hear a voice in my head.

Go, I hear the voice say. *It's not safe for you here, Caitria.* In an instant, I know it's the Cailleach. *Get to a Void before it's too late.* The warning in her voice is clear. *You know where to go.*

Chapter 21

It feels like only a few minutes when I open my eyes again. However, the light streaming through the window says otherwise. It takes a moment to adjust to the brightness. Once I can see, I carefully stand up off the floor. Looking around the room, I notice Anna isn't here anymore.

A sense of panic sets in. I stumble, tripping over a flannel on the floor. It's the same one I let her use the night before. The scarf is folded neatly on the bed. I silently hope she was well enough to go to her own room sometime in the night.

I walk toward the door, about to go up the four flights of stairs to her room, when I notice a dirt smudge on my hand. A quick glance down lets me know that I'm covered in dirt. After taking a few minutes to take a quick shower, I throw on some clean clothes before wandering out into the hallway. I get to the base of the staircase when familiar voices sound from the kitchen area. I walk over to check and see if Anna's there.

A few young women walk in the opposite direction as I slowly make my way to the kitchen. We all say a brief hello, none of us stopping for a chat. I come around the threshold and find Anna and Saoirise sitting at one of the small tables in the corner. The panic I felt earlier dissipates, only to be replaced by anxiety. I'm not sure what Anna remembers from last night. If she remembers everything, she might blame me. After all, that banshee wasn't there for her.

Her back is to me as I walk closer to the table. Saoirise sees me first and waves me over. Anna turns around, looking in my direction. I pause briefly, searching her face for anything that would let me know if she blames me. However, she immediately flings her arms around me.

"Thank goodness you're all right," Anna exclaims, and I breathe a sigh of relief. She lets me go but doesn't sit back down. "What the hell was that thing?"

"I've been telling ya," Saoirise says, standing up. "The damn thing was a banshee. I heard its shrieking."

Saoirise gives me a good look, focusing on my arms and legs. I see her visibly relax once she realizes I'm not physically injured. She pulls me in for a quick hug.

"No idea what it was doing here," Saoirise continues, gesturing for all of us to sit at the table. "Ya never see those things here."

"Wait," Anna says after a second before looking over at me after we're seated.

I shake my head, hoping she gets the message. Thankfully, she doesn't say anything. I'm not sure how much Saoirise knows, but the last thing anyone needs is to get dragged into this. I'm still not quite sure what "this" is. If what I think I heard the Cailleach say in my head is any indication, it wasn't just my parents that I should've been worried about when leaving Isle Draíocht.

"At least yer both all right," Saoirise says.

She gets up and grabs a few pastries while I heat the kettle for some tea. Once we all have a cup of tea, we silently begin eating. It's an uncomfortable silence. Anna looks over at me, suspicion in her eyes. Saoirise, on the other hand, looks between us. I fidget in my chair, unable to stay still. Saoirise excuses herself the second she's done eating. Anna looks over at me but doesn't say anything. We sit there for a few minutes, neither of us saying anything.

"I'll see you later?" she asks, breaking the silence and gathering up her dishes.

"Absolutely," I tell her, relieved she's not ignoring me.

Once she's left the room, I decide to go for a walk outside before my shift at the pub starts. Making a quick stop in my room, I throw on some shoes before going to brush my teeth. The hair on the back of my neck stands up as a slight chill runs through me. I don't think much of it until I look in the mirror. What I see has me frozen in place. There's another face in the mirror, and her bright red eyes are gleaming back at me as a cruel smile spreads across her face.

"Did you enjoy my little friend?" Carman asks as I'm unable to look away. "She was hurt you ran away. But then, you had company."

"Leave her alone," I say in a low voice. My legs begin to feel weak as she lets out a harsh laugh. I hold on to the sink to remain upright. "It's me you want."

"Dain also mentioned the girl," Carman says as her smile grows impossibly wider. "She may not have the Sight, but she has other value."

Her meaning is clear. Carman wouldn't hesitate to harm someone to get what she wants. The blood drains from my face at the thought. The first friend I've made since leaving the isle, someone who feels almost like a sister, is now in Carman's dangerous path because of me. I'm furious, both at Carman and myself. After everything I've done to try and help people, I've only made things worse for someone else. Angry tears sting my eyes.

"I'll never help you," I tell her, my voice trembling.

She cackles in response before looking back at me. In the mirror, her hand grabs my left shoulder. It stings and a burning pain seeps into my skin. I can feel her sharp fingers digging into my skin. When I look away from the mirror, she's nowhere to be seen. The pain, however, is very real. I feel sweat beginning to form on my face as I look back at Carman's reflection.

"Never say never, Caitria," she whispers menacingly, sounding like she's right next to me. "You'll find I can be quite persuasive."

I hear a knock on the door, and Carman's eyes flicker in the direction of the door.

"Soon, you'll give me your Sight," she threatens, her eyes growing even brighter. "I'll take everything from you until you do."

In the blink of an eye, she's gone. The pain in my shoulder remains. I pull aside my shirt and am frozen by what I see. My breath catches in my throat. There, marked on my skin where her fingers were, are four dark red marks. The center of each spot is almost black, with the dark red radiating out. I lightly touch one, a sharp pain shooting through my shoulder, causing me to cry out. There's another knock at the door.

"Cait?" I hear Saoirise call out from the hallway. "Everything all right?"

"Yes," I reply. I wince as I pull my shirt back in place before going to the door.

My skin feels tender, and my arm begins to tingle as I try to open the bathroom door. When I lift my left arm, though, it feels incredibly weak. However, I don't have time to think about it. If I don't leave soon, I'll be late. I throw on a clean sweater and a scarf, taking care not to touch my left shoulder as much as possible, before I head out to the hallway.

Saoirise gives me a look of concern when I open the door but stays silent. She walks me to the pub but doesn't say anything. I can tell how on edge she is. Even though it's light out and a number of people are walking around, she jumps at every little sound. I feel terrible. It's clear now that I'm putting her and Anna in danger by simply being around them. The marks on my shoulder, and how horribly Anna was impacted by the banshee, only show how real the danger is.

With each day that passes, my anxiety grows. Carman's reflection replaces my own in every single window outside, giving me a creepy, menacing smile. She doesn't speak, nor does she hurt me or anyone else. Her bright eyes have been haunting me. I've begun avoiding reflective surfaces, terrified she'll reach through and grab me. Nightmares have plagued my dreams, each one vivid and terrifying. Images of Carman torturing me to get what she wants have filled my mind.

Her sons made their own appearance. Last night, they were standing down the street, watching me. All three were present, identical with the exception of their hands. Each had their own creepy smiles. It was a horrifying scene to find as I left the pub. They all watched me silently, but none approached me. It's almost like they're waiting for something. What it is, though, I don't know.

The marks Carman left still remain. I check them every morning and night in the hopes that they'll begin healing. Much to my dismay, they've only gotten worse. The black spots at the center of each wound have grown, now shining as if I'm bleeding. Every time I try to clean them, I can hardly touch them before sharp pains cause me to double over. My veins in the area have slowly been growing dark red, creating a grotesque spiderweb growing away from my wounds. My arm has only grown weaker, and everyday movements have become more tiring.

Tom noticed it the few times I've tried to carry more than a few plates at a time. Every time, the plates have all crashed to the floor. After the third time, he must've realized that I'd be of better use not carrying much of anything. With the investigator from the isle gone, I've been more of a hostess. Even that, though, has taken so much out of me.

Saoirise's also been acting more cautious, accompanying Anna and me from the pub every night. She rarely says anything, and we're all practically silent until we get to the kitchen at the hostel. Since the run-in with the banshee, Anna and I have silently agreed to make something at the hostel every night after my shift ends. It's repetitive, but at least we're all safe. We've hardly talked about what happened, but at least we're still talking. For that alone, I'm happy.

"Anna, I know yer leaving tomorrow, but ye'll be missed," Saoirise says, holding up a pint. Anna's last night came before we knew it. We all decided to eat at the pub as soon as my shift ends to celebrate and say farewell.

"Aw, thanks, Saoirise," Anna replies with a smile, clinking their glasses together. "I'll miss you, too."

"Ya still taking Cait with ya?" she asks after taking a swig of her beer.

"I don't have the money," I say quietly before anyone else can chime in.

No matter how much Anna and I have talked about it and all the things we'll do when we get there, there's just no way I'll be able to afford it. I'd have to work for at least another few months before I'd get close to having enough money. Anna gives me a small smile, and I can tell she's trying not to cry.

"Well, this'll help," Tom says as he drops off a few plates of food.

He reaches into his back pocket and hands me a rather large, thick envelope. I open it and glance inside, surprised to find a small, flat document and a bundle of money. I open my mouth to say something, but no words come out.

"Wherever ya go, ya need a passport. And that," Saoirise says, nodding toward the envelope. "Should be enough to get a one-way ticket."

"Oh," I say, trying to find the words. "This is too much. Why? How—"

"Ya earned it," Saoirise says as she holds up her hand to cut me off before nodding toward Tom. He places a hand on her shoulder as they each give me a warm smile. "Consider it yer holiday bonus."

"Thank you," I choke out as I feel tears on my face.

Standing up, I don't hesitate to give them both a hug. Saoirise laughs in surprise, and Tom just goes along with it. Anna joins in, and we stand there, no doubt getting all sorts of looks from the other patrons. We break apart, and the three of us sit back down as Tom walks back to the bar. As he leaves, I see him wipe away tears.

"I can't believe it," Anna says after a minute. I look at her and see she's sporting a wide grin, and I smile in response before I start laughing, tears still falling from my face.

"I can come with." I laugh, wiping away my tears as more continue to fall. For the first time in a while, I'm feeling more hopeful than I've ever felt.

Chapter 22

Anna and I catch a bus to the airport bright and early the next morning. She figured out late the night before that I was much more sheltered from the world than she originally thought and decided to help prepare me for the rest of the world. The entire bus ride, she tells me all about the airport and airplanes. I receive an explanation of how boarding works, as well as what I need to know when going through security. Anna even tells me about what it's like to ride on a plane.

We moved a bit slower than either of us wanted, but the pain in my shoulder has only gotten worse. However, I try my best to ignore it, not wanting that to become a reason why we can't travel. The airport is a flurry of activity and noise as we get to the check-in desk. People walk fast around us as we wait in the line. Anna helps me buy a ticket to Seattle in the United States. I manage not to get too distracted as we make our way through the airport. Once we arrive at the gate, we each take a seat and wait for the plane to begin boarding. Too excited to rest, I sit upright and alert as I watch the people walk by.

"Are you ready for an adventure?" Anna asks excitedly.

"I feel like I've been ready for a long time," I tell her.

"Oh, good," she says with a huge smile. "I'm so excited for you to meet everyone. They're going to love you."

"You're sure?" I ask.

With everything that's happened, I completely forgot the possibility that Anna's family might not actually like me. Anxiety hits me in an instant at this new possibility. What if they meet me and actually hate me? Anna has really become like a sister, but her family is a completely different story. I've only ever heard her talk about them, and while they sound great, there's always the very real possibility that things could go terribly.

"It's going to be so exciting," she tells me as she practically starts jumping in her seat. Her smile never leaves her face. "Theo'll pick us up. I hope they told him you're coming. If not, he'll complain about needing to clean the car when we get there."

"Who's Theo?" I ask, never having heard that name from her before.

"Oh," she says, waving her hand. "He's my dad's friend's son. Kinda like the brother I never wanted."

She's about to say more when the flight attendants announce the start of the boarding process. Anna asked if we could sit next to each other when we got my ticket so we could be seatmates for the next ten hours. We slowly make our way onto the plane. It doesn't take long to find our seats. I'm about to ask more questions after they go through a safety demonstration when I realize that Anna's completely asleep.

I decided to focus on the world outside the window. It feels so surreal. The plane takes off, and I can't look away from the window. My stomach drops, and I'm immediately grateful that Anna took the time to give me a warning on what to expect. As I see the ground get further and further away, I feel a pang of sadness. I've spent my whole life here, and now I'm leaving it behind. A tear escapes and rolls down my cheek. I wipe it away as the reality hits me in a way it hadn't before. I'd been so excited about this new beginning that I didn't realize how much it'd hurt to leave it all behind. It feels like I'm losing a piece of myself.

"Ma'am?" a female voice says.

I tear my gaze away from the view and see a flight attendant. She doesn't say anything else but gives me a napkin. After she walks away, I wipe away the tears and continue looking out the window. Once we're in the clouds and I can no longer see anything, I close the window shade and try to drift off to sleep. It takes a while, but eventually, I fall asleep.

It feels like only a few minutes have passed when I'm woken up. Anna's nudging my right shoulder. Her eyes are glued to the view from the window.

"We're about to land," she tells me once I come to my senses, and she points out the window.

I look and am shocked at the number of tall buildings. I see streets and cars as far as I can see. It's like nothing I've ever imagined. In the distance are snow-capped mountains, taller than any I've ever seen. It's only a few minutes to land, but I watch the views from the window with amazement. Soon, the plane lands, and we make our way through an impossibly large and bustling airport. It takes longer than I expected, but we eventually get to a large conveyor belt where Anna picks up her large suitcase.

"I can't believe how light you packed," Anna tells me with a sigh as she struggles to roll her bag through the airport. "Theo always gives me shit for overpacking."

"That's because you wanted to backpack without a backpack," a male voice says.

We both turn around, and she rolls her eyes at the young man behind us. His blue eyes are so clear and striking that, for a second, I'm unsure whether he's human. The plaid shirt he's wearing hangs loose over his shirt and jeans.

"Yeah, yeah," Anna tells him. "Just help us with our bags, all right?"

"Who's this?" he asks, looking at me. Something about him feels so familiar, though I can't quite place why.

"This is Cait," Anna exclaims as she throws an arm around my shoulders. "Mom and Dad said she could stay with us for a while."

"Cait?" he skeptically asks as he takes both of our bags and begins walking toward the parking lot. "I thought they were talking about you bringing a pet home, not a person."

"Shut up," she says, giving him a playful smack. "Just get us home, will ya?"

"Will do," he says with a laugh and gives me a smile, showing off his dimples. "Cait, you get the front seat."

"That's not fair." Anna sighs as we get to the car.

"Yeah, well, that's tough," he tells her, grabbing my bag from my shoulder and slinging it over his own. "I'm the driver, and I say she gets the front, so you'll just have to deal with it."

"He's so annoying," she mumbles as we follow behind him.

As we climb in, I feel a rush of hopefulness. Something just feels more final. It's like I'm finally coming to the end of a long journey. I'm at the start of this new beginning and, even though it's been a new and terrifying adventure to get to this point, something about this feels right. As he pulls the car out of the lot, he looks over at me.

"'I'm Theo, by the way," he says, reaching a hand toward me.

"It's nice to meet you," I reply as I shake his hand.

"I was just joking about the whole pet thing," he tells me with an apologetic smile. My heart beats a little faster and I feel myself smile back at him. "They said Anna had a friend coming back with her."

"Anna said you'd be pretty unhappy to have to clean your car at the airport," I reply.

"You didn't," he exclaims, reaching into the back seat and tries to smack Anna's knee. "You little shit."

"Hey, it's true though," she replies, laughing at the interaction while avoiding his hand. "Now, keep it down, okay? I've gotta get my beauty sleep."

"Whatever," he says, rolling his eyes at her in the rearview mirror.

In less than a minute, she's snoring softly with her head resting on the window. He pulls onto a wide stretch of road and picks up speed. I try to sneakily grab the door handle as cars swerve among one another in front of us.

"You're safe, you know," he says, looking over at me. "I'll make sure we get home in one piece."

"Sorry," I say as I let go of the door. His words are comforting, but something about him makes me nervous.

"Why don't we play a game?" he suggests, his eyes never once leaving the road. "It'll help you get your mind off the other cars."

"All right," I say quietly. "What'd you have in mind?"

"It's a question game," Theo explains. "You ask a question, and we both answer. Then I ask a question, and we go back and forth."

"Okay," I say, nodding.

Over the next hour, Theo and I go back and forth. Soon, I completely forget to pay attention to the world around us and the cars passing by. We ask all sorts of questions, from favorite foods to funniest memories. He never asks about my family, thankfully, and I don't offer it up. Our conversation flows so naturally that I almost forget I just met him less than an hour ago. Before I realize it, we're talking and laughing.

I just want to see him smile again, I think after a while. It's a shock to even think that. My heart beats a little faster as I begin to realize that I might just like him. It's a crazy thought, and I push it aside and try to ignore it as we continue chatting. It isn't until he pulls the car onto a large boat that I begin to panic.

"Relax, Cait," he says, placing a hand over mind. The second our hands touch, I feel a warmth in my heart, and my cheeks grow warm. His hand is warm and soft, and it provides me with a sense of comfort. It's such a different sensation from what I felt when shaking his hand earlier that it comes as a shock. "We're almost there."

"Okay," I say, feeling slightly reassured.

A few more cars drive on before the boat begins to move. Theo doesn't move his hand off mine as we slowly make our way across the water. It's a calming feeling and he doesn't let go. We sit in a comfortable silence, his hand on mine, as the boat inches closer to its destination. After a short time, we begin to see land forming across the water. I feel a telltale pop and realize almost instantly why the

Cailleach brought Anna and me together. She's from a Void, just like I am.

This knowledge brings me a sense of calm I didn't expect to feel. Theo lightly squeezes my hand, giving me a wave of calmness. I may miss the isle, but in his smile and Anna's kindness as well as the knowledge that where there's a Void where I may be able to see Sorcha, Glac, and the Cailleach again, I know the one that I'm finding is going to be the best place for me.

I look out the window of the car as Theo keeps hold of my hand and try to get a better look at my new home. The trees around the shoreline look so much like Isle Draíocht. A light prickling sensation goes from my left shoulder down my arm and, with each passing second, the pain I've felt since Carman dug her fingers into me begins to dull.

As we get closer, I see a pair of golden eyes shining through one of the bushes and feel a sense of comfort. That comfort, however, is short lived as a tingling sensation goes across the back of my neck. I turn around and look out the back window at the city we're leaving behind, searching for whatever is watching me. After a second, something in the distance catches my eye. There, on the opposite shore, stands four dark figures. Even from a distance, I see a pair of bright, red, cat-like eyes filled with hatred.

Acknowledgments

A number of people made this dream a reality. I would like to extend a very special thanks to those who preordered my book: Rachel Feran, Cady Shields, Kathryn McCauley, Annye Bennett, Roxana Johnson, Nancy Hartman, Laura Bluhm, Sabra Stephens, Jacob Ambrose, Zach Garber, Karolyn Kaseberg Wenschlag, Katie Hull, Kristina Arndt-Wilson, Lora McCauley, Wendy Poole, Caroline Anderson, Sierra Wilson, Lauren Barker, Aria Hynes, Nathan Smith, Jeri Hathaway-Arndt, Karen Bock, Nathan Graves, Bill Arndt, Jake Corimer, Sharon Hunt, Tracy Arndt, Kayla Randel, Mary Ambrose, Jana Austin, Grayson Bluhm, Melissa Ambrose, Jordan Graham, Marianne Hill, Neda Kikhia, Cedee Wilson, Dalton Padgett, Zachary White, Rita Ambrose, AJ Chippendale, Kimberley Hull, Jeff Ambrose, and Madison Ambrose!

Additionally, I want to thank all my wonderful beta readers: Kathryn, Karlie, Katie, Jordan, Raymond, Madison, Meg, Kylee, Rachel, Sabra, Nathan, Lora, Mike, and Alyssa.

Of course, this could never have happened without the work and support of the amazing team at Manuscripts LLC!

I want to thank my husband, who was there for all the late nights, debilitating writer's block, and every light-bulb moment. I'd like to thank our cats for being the best furry companions and the perfect inspiration for the pucai. I also want to thank my friends and family for supporting me and encouraging me to keep writing, even when I refused to let anyone read my projects.

Finally, I would like to thank you, reader, for picking up this book.